CHILDCRAFT
THE HOW AND
WHY LIBRARY

GUIDE
AND INDEX

World Book, Inc.
a Scott Fetzer company
Chicago

Childcraft—The How and Why Library

© 2006 World Book, Inc. All rights reserved. This volume may not be reproduced in whole or in part in any form without prior written permission from the publisher.

CHILDCRAFT, CHILDCRAFT—THE HOW AND WHY LIBRARY, HOW AND WHY, WORLD BOOK and the GLOBE DEVICE are registered trademarks or trademarks of World Book, Inc.

World Book, Inc.
233 N. Michigan Avenue
Chicago, IL 60601 U.S.A.

Previous editions © 2004, 2003, 2000, 1996, 1995, 1994, 1993, 1991, 1990, 1989, 1987, 1986, 1985 World Book, Inc. © 1982, 1981, 1980, 1979, World Book-Childcraft International, Inc. © 1976, 1974, 1973, 1971, 1970, 1969, 1968, 1965, 1964 Field Enterprises Educational Corporation.

International Copyright © 2006, 2004, 2003, 2000, 1996, 1995, 1994, 1993, 1991, 1990, 1989, 1987, 1986, 1985 World Book, Inc. International Copyright © 1982, 1981, 1980, 1979 World Book-Childcraft International, Inc. International Copyright © 1976, 1974, 1973, 1971, 1970, 1969, 1968, 1965, 1964 Field Enterprises Educational Corporation.

ISBN 0-7166-5729-5 (set)
ISBN (Volume 15, Guide and Index) 0-7166-5744-9

Printed in the United States of America
5 6 7 8 9 09 08 07 06 05

For information on other World Book publications, visit our Web site at **http://www.worldbook.com**

Consultant Committee

Educational Consultants

Karol Bartlett
Educator and Science Specialist
The Children's Museum of
Indianapolis, Indiana

Phyllis Hawk, M.A.Ed.
Educator and Consultant
Hingham, Massachusetts

Monica Hughes, B.A., M.A.Ed.
Early Years Adviser and Author,
United Kingdom

Damaris Koontz, M.S.L.S.
Media Specialist and Consultant
Salem, Oregon

Ginger Kranz
Educator and Consultant
Winona, Minnesota

Dr. Margaret G. McKeown
Learning Research and
Development Center
University of Pittsburgh

Susan Roman, Ph.D.
Executive Director
Association for Library Service
to Children
American Library Association

Betty Root, M.B.E., M.Phil. (Hon.)
Former Director, Reading and
Language Information Centre,
University of Reading, United Kingdom

Staff

Vice President, Editorial
Dominic J. Miccolis

**Editor-in-Chief,
World Book, Inc.**
Paul A. Kobasa

**Executive Editor, World Book
Publishing**
Sara Dreyfuss

Editorial

**Managing Editor,
General Publishing and
Annuals**
Maureen Mostyn Liebenson

Senior Editor
Shawn Brennan

Editor
Christine Sullivan

Writers
Corinne Bergstrom
Ellen Hughes
Kathleen Kain
Mary Kayaian
Lisa Klobuchar
Patricia Ohlenroth
Anne O'Malley
Michelle Parsons
Rebecca A. Rauff
Sheri Reda
Lori Meek Schuldt
Katie Sharp
Karen Stillman
Lisa Wroble

Indexing Services
David Pofelski, *Head*

Cartographic Services
H. George Stoll, *Head*
Wayne K. Pichler

Permissions Editor
Janet T. Peterson

Editorial Assistant
Ethel Matthews

Special Consultative Services

**Subject Editors,
World Book Encyclopedia**
Brad Finger
Thomas J. Wrobel
Daniel O. Zeff

Statistical Editor
William M. Harrod

Graphics and Design

Manager
Sandra M. Dyrlund

Designer
Charlene Epple

Photographs Editor
Kathy Creech

**Production and
Administrative Support**
John Whitney

Research

Manager, Research Services
Loranne K. Shields

Senior Researchers
Cheryl Graham, *Chief Researcher*
Lynn Durbin, Senior Researcher

Library Services
Jon M. Fjortoft

Production

**Director, Manufacturing and
Pre-Press**
Carma Fazio

Manager, Manufacturing
Barbara Podczerwinski

Senior Production Manager
Madelyn Underwood

Production Manager
Anne Fritzinger

Proofreader
Anne Dillon

Text Processing
Curley Hunter
Gwendolyn Johnson

Contents

Get introduced to Childcraft *and find out how to use the set to explore the world with your child and supplement your child's schoolwork.*

Growth and Development 46

From the formative preschool years to the crucial early school years, parents and teachers play an essential role in children's lives. Learn what to expect during these stages and how to give your child the best possible start in life.

Introduction

This volume of *Childcraft* is for you, the parent, teacher, or adult caregiver of a young child. It is designed to help you to use *Childcraft* and to understand and meet the special needs of young children.

Childcraft is especially designed for children from the preschool years through the early primary years. During those years, children develop from toddlers, dependent on parents and other adults for help with basic skills, to school-age children who are active learners with friendships outside the home.

The sections of this volume offer help with specific aspects of a young child's growth and development. The first section, "Learning with *Childcraft*," explains the objectives of *Childcraft* and the organization of the set. It provides suggestions for introducing the *Childcraft* set and individual volumes to preschool and school-age children. The suggested activities are designed to capitalize on children's own interests and their curiosity about the world around them. "Learning with *Childcraft*" also contains guides for using the volumes to enrich areas of the school curriculum, such as language and literature, critical thinking, maths, science, social studies, and the arts.

The second section, "Growth and Development," outlines the physical, mental, and emotional development of young children. The first part of "Growth and Development" describes the motor skills, social development, and language development of children from 3 to 5 and from 5 to 8 years old, and the kinds of learning experiences that children in each age group need and enjoy. It also offers some helpful

ideas about dealing with special needs of children in each age group—for example, coping with the preschool child's fears or tendencies to dawdle, and helping the school-age child learn to travel between home and school safely, handle an allowance, and cope with social problems at school.

The second part of "Growth and Development," called "For Special Consideration," contains articles about subjects that may affect young children at any time, such as growing, moving, travelling, or coping with the loss of a loved family member, friend, or pet. It also contains articles about special problems that affect only some parents and teachers, such as children's physical disabilities, mental retardation, and behavioural problems. At the end of the section, you will find reprinted a simple text version of *The Convention on Rights of the Child,* adopted by the United Nations in 1989, which outlines the basic needs and rights of children worldwide.

The third section, the Index, is a comprehensive listing of subject-area content for all volumes of *Childcraft*. This index is especially helpful in locating related information on arts, sciences, technology, and growth and development in all of Volumes 1-14. If you are sharing *Childcraft* with a young child, you can use the index to find topics quickly and easily. Or, you can help a child who is reading learn to use the index to look up topics of special interest.

Obviously, no single person and no single book can provide answers and advice on all aspects of growth and development. This volume is designed to give an overall picture of the young child's needs and behaviour. The authors and editors hope that you will find it a helpful guide to understanding and meeting the needs of young children.

Learning with *Childcraft*

Childcraft is designed to meet the learning needs of preschool and early school-age children. The organization of the volumes takes into account both how young children learn and what they want to know. It also recognizes that parents, caregivers, and teachers are instrumental in introducing the world of learning to children and making it enjoyable and rewarding.

Getting to Know *Childcraft*

The best kind of learning is fun. Children have a natural curiosity about themselves and their world, and they enjoy satisfying that curiosity. *Childcraft* helps children find answers to their questions and encourages them to explore further and find more questions to answer. It is an exciting companion for an inquisitive child. In addition, *Childcraft* is an ideal assistant for the parent or teacher of any child because it provides accurate information on a wide range of topics in language that children themselves can understand.

Objectives of *Childcraft*

Childcraft is for children. These four words represent the purpose for creating *Childcraft*. The goal of *Childcraft* is to explain ideas clearly and interestingly to children, so as to challenge, stimulate, and create an appetite for more.

The creators of *Childcraft* worked to choose topics of high interest to children from preschool (nursery school) through the primary school years. They chose stories and poems from folk literature, the classics, and the best of today's literature for children. They researched topics in nature, the sciences, the arts, and social studies—topics that parents and teachers consider significant. Then they organized the material in volumes centred around children's interests and filled with simple, direct writing and informative, exciting photography and art.

Childcraft and Children's interests

Childcraft is designed to satisfy both young children's need to know and their need to explore and understand the world of imagination and feelings. Volumes 1 and 2 nourish a child's imagination with the best of children's stories and poems—selections that help children become more aware and understanding of themselves and others. Volumes 3–14 explore the outside world, developing basic concepts and adding supporting information for children. Each volume builds on the child's knowledge and interests and points towards further learning.

In Volumes 3–14, the writers of *Childcraft* have used a style that lets children enjoy the language while learning the facts. The writing is conversational and direct, with a natural rhythm. Unfamiliar words are introduced and explained either in the selection itself or in a glossary at the end of the volume.

The illustrations are colourful and appealing. Children will find charts and diagrams that clarify the text as well as illustrations and photographs that stimulate emotional responses.

Childcraft and developmental needs

Childcraft is designed both to satisfy children and to meet the needs of parents, teachers, and other caring adults in a child's life. Adults who use *Childcraft* will find a wealth of information, literature, and activities for a range of ages.

This section of the *Guide and Index*, "Learning with *Childcraft*," provides you with an overview of content, together with suggestions for introducing and using specific volumes at home and in the classroom. Two articles that follow, "Introducing *Childcraft* to Children" and "Curriculum enrichment," together with the tables of contents and indexes of the individual volumes, will help you guide children to the books and pages that have the right information.

Organization of *Childcraft*

The first two volumes of *Childcraft* introduce children to literature from all ages and from around the world. In volumes 3–14, children learn about living things, machines and numbers, stars and planets, the arts, the world and its people, and themselves. Volume 15 contains articles on child development for parents and teachers.

In Volumes 3–14, most material is presented as two-page articles. Each of these volumes includes a subject index.

Description of Contents

Volume 1 **Poems and Rhymes**

This volume contains selections to read aloud and share with young children—nursery rhymes, poems, and proverbs. Throughout this volume, you'll find classic Mother Goose rhymes, translated rhymes from many countries and cultures, and many other fun poems to read.

The selections are arranged into five sections—"For Fun," which has a wide variety of subjects; "Things to Know," which introduces the alphabet, counting rhymes, and poems about other concepts; "Animals Only," which focuses on rhymes about animals; "Just Play," which is full of finger rhymes, skipping-rope rhymes, and tongue twisters; and "Wise Words," which is a selection of fables and proverbs from around the world.

Volume 2 **Once Upon a Time**

The second volume features selections for children who are beginning to enjoy fairy tales, folk tales, and stories. Many familiar classics are included, such as "Jack and the Beanstalk," "The Emperor's New Clothes," and "Cinderella," along with examples from many countries, including the African tale "Why Mosquitoes Buzz in People's Ears".

The selections are grouped into three sections—"Fairy Tales," "Folk Tales and Legends," and "Stories and Excerpts".

Volume 3 **Art Around Us**

The third volume encourages children to learn about different forms of art and how to create art with objects they find around them. Throughout this volume, children are shown how to use odds and ends such as paper clips and flower petals as well as paints, clay, papier mâché, and fabrics to create works of art. They are also introduced to great representatives of the arts— Prokofiev, Shakespeare, Michelangelo and many others.

This volume is arranged in five sections—"Craftwork," "Let's Paint," "Statues and Sculptures," "Music to Your Ears," and "Theatre".

Volume 4 **The World of Animals**

Mammals, birds, fish, reptiles, amphibians, and other animals are featured, along with explanations of the characteristics of each group, how animals fit into the web of life, and how animals and people affect each other.

This volume has eight general chapters, including "What Is an Animal?" "Amazing Animals," and "Animals in Danger," as well as five chapters explaining seven different classes of animals.

Volume 5 **The World of Plants**

As well as teaching the facts of plant life, the fifth volume focuses on how important plants are to us— how we use them for food and to make paper, cloth, even buildings and medicine. The text also demonstrates how important it is that people, in turn, should look after the world of plants.

"The Life of a Plant," "Nature's Neighbours," "What Plants Do for Us," "How Does your Garden Grow?" and "Plants Need Help, Too" are the five sections that make up this volume.

Volume 6 **Our Earth**

The sixth book describes the dramatic phenomena of the earth's activities and stimulates children's interest in their own environment. The volume approaches the subject process by process, describing each topic in a strongly visual manner.

Starting with "Planet Earth," then moving through "Land on the Earth," "Oceans, Lakes, and Rivers," "Air, Wind, and Clouds," and "Weather," Volume 6 leaves us contemplating "Why Protect the Earth?" and "How Can People Protect the Earth?"

Volume 7 **The Universe**

In this book about astronomy, the sun, Earth's moon, and each planet of the solar system are dealt with in detail. Then the text moves beyond the solar system into the stars and galaxies of the universe. The physical aspects of astronomy, the applications of space technology, and research in the field of communications are also discussed.

The five chapters of this volume are "The Sun," "The Moon," "Our Solar System," "The Stars," and "Studying the Universe".

Volume 8 **How Does It Happen?**

This book helps satisfy children's curiosity about basic principles of science. Simple text and generous illustrations help children understand the interaction of matter and energy in the world around them.

Divided into eight sections, including "What Happens with Machines?" and "What Makes Things Move?" this volume also tackles matter, energy, heat and cold, light, sound, and electricity.

Volume 9 **How Things Work**

The ninth volume applies the concepts discussed in *How Does It Happen?* to everyday tools and machines, giving clear and practical demonstrations of the principles introduced. In addition, this volume underlines the value of raw materials. Children will gain a greater appreciation of the application of science and the importance of technology in our everyday lives.

The five sections in this volume are "Inventions in the Home," which tackles such inventions as refrigerators and computers; "On the Move," which covers machines such as escalators, cars, and rockets; "Signals in the Air," which explores the workings of such inventions as satellites, radios, and television; "Raw Materials," which explains how everyday items from cheese to paper and plastics are made; and "Creating and Designing," which talks about the structures of houses and bridges as well as the functions of robots in manufacturing things.

Volume 10 **Shapes and Numbers**

This book entertains and challenges young readers with stories, puzzles, games, tricks, and facts about shapes and numbers. It explores such topics as how we can play and work with numbers, and where numbers came from.

The chapters in this volume are "Fun with Shapes," "The Story of Numbers," "Making Numbers Count," "Number Fun," "More Number Fun," and "Ways of Measuring".

Volume 11 **About You**

This book answers questions of special interest to young children— questions about how people are alike and different, the parts of the human body and how they work, and what feelings are. Particularly complex subjects are explained in simple language with colourful illustrations to highlight and further clarify the text.

Beginning with "Outside of You," this volume also has chapters called "Inside of You," "Your Senses," "Growing and Changing," "Thoughts and Feelings," and "Taking Care of Yourself".

Volume 12 **Who We Are**

This volume explores the many likenesses and differences in people and cultures around the world— ways of life, beliefs and customs, food, games, and education.

This book is divided into five sections—"Families and Neighbours," "What Do We Eat?" "What Games Do We Play?" "How Do We Learn Things?" and "How Do We All Get Along?"

Volume 13 **See the World**

This book describes the continents, the ways people get around, and how to use maps and plan a trip. In addition, this volume introduces children to some of the most famous places in our world. Castles, natural and historic "wonders of the world," famous skyscrapers, and national monuments, along with many other well-known places, are shown in bright illustrations and photographs that will captivate a young child's imagination.

The six chapters in this volume are "Continents of the World," "How Will You Get There?" "Where in the World?" "Famous Places," "How Do You Find Your Way?" and "Taking a Trip".

Volume 14 Celebrate!
In this book, children learn how people celebrate all over the world and discover that every month of the year there is a celebration somewhere in the world. Children also can look up their birthdays in this volume to find out what famous historical figures were born on the same date.

This book starts with "What's a Celebration?" followed by a chapter for each month of the year, highlighting some of that month's holidays and birthdays.

Volume 15 Guide and Index
This volume for parents and teachers outlines a child's growth and development from birth through the preteen years and explores issues of special concern. The volume includes suggestions for introducing and using *Childcraft*; articles about child development; and suggestions for coping with common illnesses, travelling with young children, and other special circumstances; as well as the general index for the entire series. The sections are "Learning with *Childcraft*," "A Child's Growth and Development from Three Years to Eight," and "Index".

Introducing *Childcraft* to Children

Through using *Childcraft,* children and parents alike come to love and appreciate it as a good friend. It reflects children's interests, recognizes the importance of the relationship between parent and child, and provides a stimulating way to learn.

Childcraft's effectiveness at home depends largely on how it is presented and used. It's important that you get to know *Childcraft* before introducing it to your child. If you browse through each volume, it will be easy for you to share it enthusiastically with your child.

Sharing pictures and stories from *Childcraft* is a natural way to introduce a young child to each volume of the set. These pages offer you suggestions for exploring *Childcraft* as a whole and exploring individual volumes with your child.

Preschool

BIRTH–3. This is the time to introduce *Childcraft* to your children. Set aside 15 or 20 minutes each day to share *Childcraft* with your child. This time period can vary—infants and toddlers have short attention spans, and it's important not to overdo it. Sharing *Childcraft* will help to stimulate an infant's mind and reinforce the toddler's newly acquired ability to talk.

Poems and Rhymes is specially geared to infants and toddlers. Your enthusiastic, animated presentation of rhymes and poems will encourage your child to imitate sounds and actions. With reassurance and guidance, your child can sharpen skills. Counting and action rhymes will help toddlers learn basic counting and language. Encourage your child to join in!

Ages 3–4. The transition to the preschool years is marked by an expanded vocabulary, a longer attention span, and a preoccupation with fantasy and role-playing. A 4-year-old's complete openness to learning makes sharing *Childcraft* a really rewarding experience for both parent and child.

Although most 4-year-olds can't read words, they can "read" pictures to create or re-create their own stories. They love to talk about stories that are read to them. Allow time for your child to respond and question. There's no need to hurry to the end of the story unless your child wants to. Frequent pauses to discuss pictures or passages will enable your child to re-create the story in his or her own way.

Preschool children enjoy browsing through *Childcraft* on their own, so now is the time to teach your child how to care for books. Your child will try to imitate almost everything you do, so if you treat books with care and respect, your child will quickly learn to do the same.

The bright photos and illustrations in *Childcraft* will stimulate interest. Often, your child will want feedback on the wonders in *Childcraft*. The clear, simple text will help you respond to questions in terms your child will understand.

School Age

Ages 5–7. As soon as children learn to read, their involvement with *Childcraft* will broaden, and they will start to read alone. Indeed, they will begin to explore more and more of *Childcraft* on their own.

During their first year of school, most children will continue to need some adult help in exploring *Childcraft*. In the second or third year, however, they will begin to make more use of the book without parental help. The first two volumes hold material for the reading level of this important age group. This is also an age when children become intensely curious about themselves, so the volume *About You* becomes especially important.

Place the books where your child can see them and reach them easily. Make it clear that your child can use these books at any time, but also is responsible for looking after them. This, too, is part of the learning process.

Free access to *Childcraft* will bolster a growing sense of competence and independence. Children will also find in *Childcraft* references to material they come across at school. If they've enjoyed *Childcraft* in their early years, they will easily develop the habit of checking *Childcraft* for information they need.

Ages 7-10. Children are often intrigued by differences in lifestyles. The volumes entitled *Who We Are* and *See the World* show the different ways people live, in what kinds of houses they live, what they eat, and fascinating examples of customs around the world. So children can go off on any tangent they choose—one element will always lead to another. They will learn that there is no limit to knowledge, if they are encouraged to pursue it.

Since most of the volumes relate to school subjects, *Childcraft* is a superb home reference library for children in primary school. Children will find material in *Childcraft* that will help them complete school assignments. *Childcraft* will help with homework problems and will still be a pleasurable experience.

During the primary-school years, children's attention tends to focus on other children. The codes, styles, and expectations of other children in the same age group will determine a great deal of each child's behaviour. The familiar practice of sharing *Childcraft* with a parent may shift to sharing *Childcraft* with a friend or group of friends. The important thing is that *Childcraft* should remain a source of enjoyment and information.

Volume 1 *Poems and Rhymes* and Volume 2 *Once Upon a Time*

Reading to your child is a wonderful way to share a close, loving relationship, for it is a time of pleasure for both of you. Your child is learning that a book holds a world of wonder and enjoyment.

At the same time, your child is learning that those strange black lines on the pages are the source of the words you speak and that someday he or she will be able to read those words, too. He or she is also discovering that you are reading from left to right and from top to bottom. And think about the pictures your child studies so intently. The realization that the flat apple on the page represents a real, rounded apple he or she can hold is an enormous leap in comprehension.

Story time provides opportunities to improve vocabulary and develop readiness for reading. Many studies have shown the connection between reading to children and their success in learning basic reading skills. So, as you read, talk about the story and answer your child's questions about letters, sounds, and words.

Before you read any story or poem to your child, read it, or at least skim it, yourself. Ask yourself: Will this interest my child? Will he or she understand what is happening? What unfamiliar words or ideas might I have to explain? Is this a good bedtime story, or should I read it at some other time?

Preschool

Activity 1. No child is too young to be read to. Many educators recommend reading short, simple rhymes to infants a few weeks old. Read from the "For Fun" section of *Poems and Rhymes*. Your baby will respond to the rhythm of the words and the sound of your voice. Play with your child's hands, fingers, or toes as your read "Pat-a-Cake" or "This Little Piggy". This is fun for your baby and will soon draw smiles. These happy responses establish patterns for later learning.

Activity 2. Introduce Volume 1 to your child by reading one or two nursery rhymes. Put your finger under the words as you read them to help your child make an association between spoken and written words. Repeat each rhyme so that your child can learn part or all of it and recite it with you. If there are pictures illustrating the rhyme, point them out and talk about them with your child. In later sessions, as your child's attention span increases, go on to the other types of poetry and to the shorter tales and stories.

One for the Money
Mother Goose

One for the money,
And two for the show,
Three to get ready,
And four to go.

One for Anger
Mother Goose

One for anger,
Two for mirth,
Three for a wedding,
Four for a birth,
Five for rich,
Six for poor,
Seven for a witch,
I can tell you no more.

Mirth means fun and laughter.

Seven Blackbirds in a Tree
Mother Goose

Seven blackbirds in a tree,
Count them and see what they be.
One for sorrow
Two for joy
Three for a girl
Four for a boy
Five for silver
Six for gold
Seven for a secret
That's never been told.

1, 2, 3, 4, 5!
Mother Goose

1, 2, 3, 4, 5!
I caught a hare alive;
6, 7, 8, 9, 10!
I let her go again.

1, 2, 3, 4
Mother Goose

1, 2, 3, 4,
Mary at the cottage door;
5, 6, 7, 8,
Eating cherries off a plate.

Activity 3. Continue to read nursery rhymes to your toddler, but try some simple stories in *Once Upon a Time,* too, like "Mother, Mother, I Want Another" or "It's My Birthday". If necessary, shorten the tales and use your own words to tell simplified versions that still match the pictures. As you read, point to characters and objects in the pictures.

Activity 4. For children 3 to 5, you will be able to read complete stories. Most children in this age group will enjoy a short folk tale or fairy tale, such as "Why the Bear Has a Stumpy Tail" from *Once Upon a Time* or "The Lion and the Mouse" from *Poems and Rhymes*.

This is also a good time to use the section "Things to Know" in *Poems and Rhymes*. Here are rhymes about many of the concepts you'll want your child to understand before school begins—the alphabet, numbers from 1 to 10, days of the week, colours, and good manners.

School Age

Activity 1. Now is the time to look for stories with a more complex turn of plot, such as "Cinderella," "Jack and the Beanstalk," and "Why Mosquitoes Buzz in People's Ears". If a story is too long for one sitting, read just a few pages at a time. Look for poems, too, that match your child's special interests.

Activity 2. At 7, most children can read easy stories. This, however, does not mean that you should stop reading aloud. Reading aloud gives you a chance to whet your child's appetite for some of the great classics for children in *Once Upon a Time*. After your child has begun reading, help him or her begin using *Poems and Rhymes* independently, even while you continue reading aloud. For example, read to your child one of the long story poems, such as "Three Little Kittens" on pages 96–97, "The Fox Went Out on a Chilly Night" on pages 120–125, and "The Owl and the Pussycat" by Edward Lear on pages 130–131. Then point out that most of the poems in *Poems and Rhymes* are much shorter than the one you read and that your child may be able to read some of them. Turn to "Things to Know" on pages 52–91. Point out that almost all the words in these poems are easy to read. Encourage your child to try reading the poems.

Activity 3. If your child is developing strong reading skills, take time to look through Volume 1 with him or her. Note that this is where the nursery rhymes and other poems are found. Also look through *Once Upon a Time* with your child and point out the easiest stories, such as "The Little Red Hen," on pages 90–92, and "Mother, Mother, I Want Another," by Maria Polushkin, on pages 140–147. Let your child choose a short poem and read it to you. Encourage your child to read other poems and stories alone.

Activity 4. Browse through the stories in *Once Upon a Time* with your child and get him or her to predict from the pictures what each story is about. Ask which stories look most interesting and why. Help your child find stories that are comfortable reading and choose one to read. Get your child to read the first paragraph or so aloud to you and finish reading the story independently. Encourage your child to go on to others.

Activity 5. Your child may be interested in stories in *Once Upon a Time* that are beyond his or her reading level. Don't forget that even though children are reading on their own, they still enjoy being read to. When your child seems interested in a story but cannot read it alone, read it aloud slowly, following the text with your finger so your child can follow along.

It's My Birthday
by Helen Oxenbury

"It's my birthday and I'm going to make a cake. I need some eggs."

"It's my birthday and I'm going to make a cake."

"I'll get you some eggs," said the chicken.

148

149

WORLD BOOK'S CHILDCRAFT
ONCE UPON A TIME

Volume 3 *Art Around Us*

Preschool

Activity 1. Prepare to introduce Volume 3, *Art Around Us,* by previewing pages 12–13 to learn what types of materials are needed for the easy crafts and activities in this book. Then, with your child, look through the pages and choose one of the projects. Help your child with the directions if necessary. Then talk about what materials to collect for other projects, where to store them, where to work on the projects, and how to clean up.

Activity 2. Pick a chapter in the book in which your child would be especially interested. Flip through the pages of this chapter with your child, looking at and discussing the pictures. Talk to your child about examples of these art forms in everyday life, such as a painting or figurine in your home. Talk about a puppet show your child saw and compare it to the theatre.

School Age

Activity 1. Read through the chapter called "Music to Your Ears" with your child and make a list of the types of music your child finds most interesting. Then take your child to your local library to find recordings of these types and some others. Listen to the music at home together and talk about what your child likes in each style.

Activity 2. Read about puppets with your child on pages 166–169. Then help your child make one or two puppets using the instructions on pages 170–173. Ask your child to think of a simple story to act out as a puppet show.

Getting Crafty

To do all the crafts in this chapter, you will need lots of materials. Some things you will need for only one project. But other things you will use again and again.

It is a good idea to collect the materials listed on page 13 and keep them in a large cardboard box. Then you will have the materials you need to work with.

Where will you find your materials? You may have to buy some at a craft store. But you can start your collecting at home and outside. Remember to get permission before you add something to your collection. And be careful when handling sharp objects.

Craft materials to collect
- rubber bands
- tracing paper
- bowls of different sizes
- cardboard
- clear tape
- crayons
- glue
- flowers
- leaves
- food coloring
- heavyweight and lightweight paper in different colors
- magazines
- markers
- masking tape
- newspaper
- open-weave canvas
- pencils
- pieces of cloth
- a ruler
- scissors
- streamers
- string
- tissue paper
- wax paper
- embroidery hoop
- embroidery needle
- embroidery thread

WORLD BOOK'S CHILDCRAFT
ART AROUND US

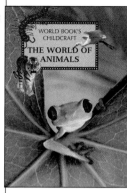

Animals Eat

All plants and all animals need food. Most plants make their own food from light, water, and **substances** in the ground and air. But animals cannot make their own food. They must eat plants or other animals to live.

Different kinds of animals eat in different kinds of ways. A chameleon (kuh MEE lee uhn) flips out its sticky tongue and catches insects. A lammergeier, a type of vulture, uses its sharp claws and hooked beak to tear its food.

A butterfly has a mouthpart like a built-in straw. It's called a proboscis (proh BAHS ihs). The butterfly keeps its proboscis rolled up until it gets hungry. Then it unrolls its proboscis, puts it into a flower, and sucks up sweet nectar.

African lammergeier

12

butterfly

A ground squirrel has strong teeth for cracking nuts and seeds. It carries food home in its cheeks and "squirrels" it away.

A baleen whale fills its mouth with seawater. The water is full of tiny plants and animals. The whale lets the water run out of its mouth. Then it swallows the plants and animals that remain.

South American giant anteater

raccoon

KNOW HOW What's for dinner? Animals can be grouped by what they eat. Some animals eat only plants. They are called herbivores. Herbivores include cattle, sheep, and squirrels. Animals that eat only other animals are called carnivores. Carnivores include lions, foxes, and snakes. Animals that eat both plants and animals are called omnivores. Omnivores include bears, raccoons, hogs, and human beings. What do you think animals that eat only insects are called? Right! Insectivores. Anteaters and hedgehogs are insectivores.

king cobra

golden-mantled ground squirrel

WORLD BOOK'S CHILDCRAFT
THE WORLD OF ANIMALS

Volume 4 *The World of Animals*

Preschool

Activity 1. Explain that Volume 4, *The World of Animals,* shows how animals belong in groups. Turn to the table of contents and read the eight chapter titles to your child. Then invite your child to choose one chapter to find out what the title means. Turn to the first two pages, read them, and talk about the illustration. Encourage your child to talk about what he or she sees on these pages.

Activity 2. Point out many other colourful and informative pictures throughout the volume. Encourage your child to look at the pictures just for fun and to find out about animals of all types. Also encourage your child to bring any questions he or she may have to you.

School Age

Activity 1. Explain that people who study animals put animals that are alike into groups. Explain that several chapters in *The World of Animals* are about different animal groups. Read the title and introduction of any chapter opener to your child. Invite your child to choose a chapter and to browse through the articles and pictures independently.

Activity 2. Ask your child to name a favourite animal. Use the index to find pages of *The World of Animals* that discuss or illustrate the animals. If there is a picture, help your child read the caption.

Invite your child to name other favourite animals. Use the index to help your child find the pages that have pictures or text about them.

Where It's Always Dry

A desert seems like a tough place for plants to live. There's little water, and the ground is hard and dry. But many plants and animals survive in deserts.

It doesn't rain often in a desert. And when it does, the ground dries quickly. So the roots of most desert plants spread far out just below the surface of the ground. The plants' roots can then catch every drop of water that falls. Most desert plants store up all the water they can get.

During the day, the desert looks lifeless. Most desert animals hide where they can escape the sun's heat—under a rock, underground, or even in a hole in a cactus.

When the sun goes down, a desert quickly cools. Desert rodents look for seeds. Lizards hunt insects. Snakes hunt the rodents and lizards.

It sometimes rains in a desert. When it does, the desert bursts into bloom because there are many seeds in most deserts. But almost all of these plants quickly wither and die as the ground dries again.

During the day, the desert looks hot and lifeless.

As the sun goes down, the desert cools and bursts into life.

WORLD BOOK'S CHILDCRAFT
THE WORLD OF PLANTS

Volume 5 *The World of Plants*

Preschool

Activity 1. Read the title of Volume 5, *The World of Plants,* and explain that the book is about plants of all kinds. Look through the volume for a plant that your child is familiar with. Get your child to look at the picture as you read the text. Let your child browse through the book to enjoy the pictures.

Activity 2. Introduce *The World of Plants* as a reference source. Explain that the book tells you about all kinds of plants. Look through the book and point out some of the most interesting plants. Encourage your child to look at the pictures in the rest of the book for fun. If your child has questions about the pictures, read some of the text to find answers.

School Age

Activity 1. Turn to one of the four-page articles in the chapter "Nature's Neighbours" on pages 54–87. Read the pages with your child and look at and talk about the pictures, then read the text. Let your child look through the rest of the book and use pictures, captions, and titles to preview the content.

Activity 2. If you have a globe or map of the world, use it as you and your child look through *The World of Plants.* Turn to the article on pages 156–157. Ask your child to choose a favourite. Then find its location on the globe or map. Point out where you live and the land and water between you and the place your child picked. Discuss how you would get there.

Volume 6 *Our Earth*

Preschool

Activity 1. Some topics in *Our Earth* address questions in every child's early life, such as "What makes the wind blow?" or "Why is the sky blue?" *Our Earth* answers some of these questions.

Introduce *Our Earth* in short sessions. Let your child find a two-page article with an interesting picture. Read the title and ask your child what the picture shows. Then read the article aloud or explain it simply. Limit the activity to 10 minutes.

Activity 2. Let your child look at pictures in the book whenever he or she feels like it and bring questions about them to you for explanations.

School Age

Activity 1. Your child may be ready to read picture labels and captions. Turn to a page with an easy-to-read caption, such as page 10, 77, 80, or 139. After you talk with your child about the illustration, read the caption aloud. Then encourage your child to read it. Compliment your child for correct or approximate readings. Let your child try reading other captions.

Activity 2. Encourage independent reading by helping your child do an experiment, such as "What Is Air Made Of?" (pages 108–109) or "How Does Air Push?" (pages 110–111). With your child, talk about the pictures, read the text, and work on the experiment together.

Volume 7 The Universe

Preschool

Activity 1. This volume deals with the sun, moon, and stars as well as the solar system, space, and space travel. Introduce *The Universe* by sharing such information as "Why Does the Sun Disappear at Night?" (pages 18–19), "Why Does the Moon Shine?" (pages 46–47), or "What Are Stars?" (pages 100–101). Look at the pictures with your child and read the article or explain as much information as your child wants to know.

Activity 2. Ask your child to name some things the sun does, such as that it rises and sets, gives off light and makes things warm. Then look at the pictures for "Why Is the Sun Important?" (pages 14–17) and read the text or explain it simply. Use the pictures to follow energy from the sun to plants, animals, and people.

School Age

Activity 1. With your child, compare the photographs of the sun (page 11) and moon (page 40). Talk about the two photos: Does the sun look as hard and rocky as the moon? Does the moon look as hot as the sun? Then ask your child to find a photo of a planet in Chapter 3, "Our Solar System". Talk about whether the planet might be hot or cold, rocky or made of softer things, like water or clouds. Then read about the planet with your child.

Activity 2. Read "Star Pictures" (pages 108–109) with your child. Then let your child choose and read some of the "Star Stories" (pages 110–113). With your child, look for some of the constellations mentioned in "Finding Star Pictures" (pages 114–117).

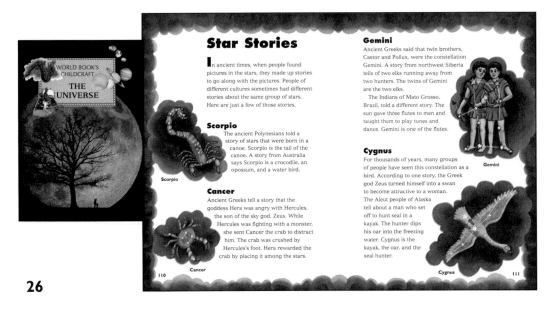

Star Stories

In ancient times, when people found pictures in the stars, they made up stories to go along with the pictures. People of different cultures sometimes had different stories about the same group of stars. Here are just a few of those stories.

Scorpio
The ancient Polynesians told a story of stars that were born in a canoe. Scorpio is the tail of the canoe. A story from Australia says Scorpio is a crocodile, an opossum, and a water bird.

Cancer
Ancient Greeks tell a story that the goddess Hera was angry with Hercules, the son of the sky god, Zeus. While Hercules was fighting with a monster, she sent Cancer the crab to distract him. The crab was crushed by Hercules's foot. Hera rewarded the crab by placing it among the stars.

Gemini
Ancient Greeks said that twin brothers, Castor and Pollux, were the constellation Gemini. A story from northwest Siberia tells of two elks running away from two hunters. The twins of Gemini are the two elks.
The Indians of Mato Grosso, Brazil, told a different story. The sun gave three flutes to men and taught them to play tunes and dance. Gemini is one of the flutes.

Cygnus
For thousands of years, many groups of people have seen this constellation as a bird. According to one story, the Greek god Zeus turned himself into a swan to become attractive to a woman. The Aleut people of Alaska tell about a man who set off to hunt seal in a kayak. The hunter dips his oar into the freezing water. Cygnus is the kayak, the oar, and the seal hunter.

WORLD BOOK'S CHILDCRAFT
THE UNIVERSE

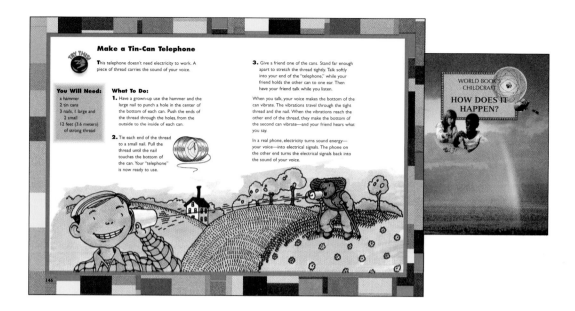

Volume 8 *How Does It Happen?*

Preschool

Activity 1. Introduce Volume 8, *How Does It Happen?,* to your child by reading "The Fire Bringer" on pages 104–111. Talk about fire with your child, its many uses as well as its dangers.

Activity 2. Read "Energy from Movement" (pages 66–67) to your child and talk about how making something move gives it energy. Let your child think of some examples, such as pushing a swing, throwing a ball, or pushing a pushchair. Then let your child try the domino activity (page 66) and see how the energy from pushing one domino travels down the whole row.

School Age

Activity 1. Read "Hard, Wet, and Invisible" (pages 58–59) with your child. Let your child name some familiar things that are solid, liquid, and gas. Then invite your child to read some of the riddles in "Mealtime Matter" (pages 60–63) and name the foods described.

Activity 2. Help your child make the tin-can telephone described on pages 146–147. After building and using the "phone," read the text on pages 138–145 with your child about sound and how it travels. Talk about the vibrations of the string, which take the sound from one can to the other.

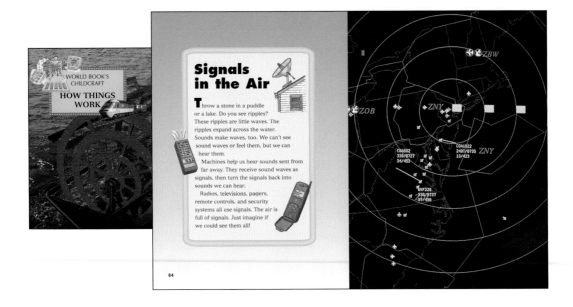

Volume 9 *How Things Work*

Preschool

Activity 1. Choose an easy (level 1) project in Volume 9, *How Things Work,* and collect the materials for it. Then read the title of the book and look through it with your child to see what it is about. Look at the project, read the directions, and do the project together. Talk about just as much of the principle—for example, wind, power, or heat—as you think your child will understand.

Activity 2. Read "Great Idea!" (pages 12–13) in Chapter 1, "Inventions in the Home," to your child. Let your child look through the chapter and find pictures of things people use at home. Then ask your child to think of a new invention to use at home, draw a picture of it, and explain what it does.

School Age

Activity 1. This activity will give your child practice in grouping and classifying. With your child, look through Chapter 2, "On the Move," and find pictures of things that move on land, in water, in the air, and underground. Then let your child name other categories, such as "machines that move people" and "machines that move things," and find some examples of each.

Activity 2. Read the introduction to Chapter 3, "Signals in the Air" (pages 84–85) with your child. Help your child think of some things that work by using signals. Then look through the chapter for examples. Let your child choose one that looks interesting and read the article about it alone or with your help.

Volume 10 *Shapes and Numbers*

Preschool

Activity 1. Introduce Volume 10, *Shapes and Numbers,* by reading one of the stories included in the volume, such as "The Farmer's Square" (pages 20–23) or "The Foolish Millionaire and the Clever Girl" (pages 122–125).

Activity 2. Play "Shape Tangle" (from pages 30–31) with your child. Not only is this game good for teaching shapes, but it also helps your child learn body parts and learn *left* and *right*. Get your child to help you make the shapes. As you cut them out, tell your child their names. If just two of you play, take turns being the "caller". Play slowly and encourage your child to think before moving. If your child makes a mistake, give gentle encouragement and help to get it right.

School Age

Activity 1. With your child, work out the answers to your choice of these puzzlers in Volume 10: "Disappearing Squares" (pages 18–19); "Polyominoes" (pages 24–25); and "The Magic Number in Your Name" (pages 96–97).

Activity 2. Explain that *Shapes and Numbers* describes many ways to think about and work with numbers. Read the table of contents, then turn to one or more of these articles to explore some maths concepts in simple terms: "What's the Biggest Number" (pages 106–107), "The Magic of Multiplication" (pages 110–111), and "What Is Measuring?" (pages 158–159). Depending on your child's reading ability, read the text aloud or help him or her to read.

The Farmer's Square

Long ago, there was a farmer whose land was in the shape of a square. Each side of the square was exactly 100 paces long.

One day, a tired, dusty man knocked at the farmer's door and asked for something to eat. The kind farmer gave him a nice lunch.

After the man had eaten, he said, "Farmer, I am your king! As a reward for your kindness, you may double the size of your land. But after you add the new land, your farm must still be in the shape of a square."

The farmer was overjoyed. He went out at once to **measure** his new land and put a fence around it.

At first the farmer thought the sides of the new square should be 200 paces long—twice as long as the sides of the old square. But this plan didn't work. The square he measured was four times as big as his old farm!

21

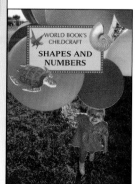

WORLD BOOK'S CHILDCRAFT

SHAPES AND NUMBERS

Do your parents tell you to cover your nose and mouth when you sneeze? That's because when you sneeze, tiny drops of fluid spray out of your mouth. Tiny germs travel in that fluid and can make other people sick too.

What Happens When You Get Sick?

Have you had chickenpox or measles, a cold, an ear infection, or the flu? If so, your body was under attack!

When you get sick, tiny germs called viruses (VY ruhs uhz) or bacteria (bak TEER ee uh) attack your body. Some of these germs travel from person to person in the drops of fluid that shoot out of the mouth during a sneeze or cough. Some

are spread in food and water. These germs can make you feel sick.

Luckily your body fights back. And sometimes medicine helps your body fight the germs.

After you have been sick with certain illnesses, your body remembers the germs. If one of the germs tries to attack again, your body destroys it as soon as it enters your body. That's why you usually get some illnesses, like chickenpox, only once.

You can get some illnesses, like colds and the flu, over and over again. This is because there are so many kinds of cold and flu viruses. If a new virus invades your body, your body does not know that virus, and so you get sick.

Volume 11 *About You*

Preschool

Activity 1. Explain that Volume 11, *About You,* is about growing and taking care of oneself. Turn to "Thoughts and Feelings" on pages 114–143. Look at and talk about the photographs that show activities, moods, emotions, relationships with friends and family members, and curiosity about the future.

Activity 2. The first half of "Growing and Changing" (pages 92–101) is useful for answering the typical question, "Where did I come from?" The pictures illustrate the development of a baby and the life of a newborn infant, and the text gives enough information to satisfy a child's curiosity. Read and talk about this section with your child when you feel the time is right.

School Age

Activity 1. Read and talk about a high-interest article, such as "Your Growing Bones" (pages 102–103), "Families" (pages 108–111), or "What Happens When You Get Sick?" (pages 146–147). Talk about the article with your child and relate it to his or her own life.

Activity 2. If your child is interested in learning about parts of the body, give him or her a preview of the contents of Volume 11. Point out sections about muscles and bones, the respiratory system, the heart and circulatory system, the digestive system, the brain and nervous system, the sensory organs, and so on. Look at some of the pictures together. Read together and talk about any text that interests your child.

Volume 12 *Who We Are*

Preschool

Activity 1. Volume 12, *Who We Are,* is packed with colourful pictures that a young child can enjoy. Open the book to pages 4–5. Read page 5 aloud or reword the text in simpler language. Briefly discuss the pictures on page 4 with your child. Explain that the rest of the book tells more about how people around the world do things. Encourage your child to look through the book to see how people live, eat, play, learn, and enjoy life.

Activity 2. Pick a chapter with familiar activities, such as "What Games Do We Play?" Talk about what the people in the pictures are doing, and let your child guess what the chapter is about. Read the captions of pictures that interest your child. Then let your child browse through the book.

School Age

Activity 1. *Who We Are* discusses food, games, toys, education, and other aspects of many cultures. Choose an interesting article, read it with your child, and talk about the pictures. Children sometimes reject or laugh at an unfamiliar way of life. Your acceptance of other people's ways will help interest your child in learning more. Encourage your child to look through the volume.

Activity 2. Use a globe or map when you introduce *Who We Are.* Look at pictures with your child, pointing out the names of countries. Find the countries on the globe or map. Help your child understand that people in different places do things in different ways. Help your child read an interesting article and locate the countries in the article on the globe or map.

On the Playground

Sidewalk games are fun! The names may change, but the games are pretty much the same on playgrounds, sidewalks, and fields all over the world.

Do you play hopscotch? Children all over the world play it. In China, hopscotch is called *Gat Fei Gei,* which means "One-Foot Jumping Flying Machine." In Italy, it's called the *Bell.* In Austria, it's the *Temple.* In Myanmar, children squat with hands on their hips as they jump the squares.

These children in Mexico are playing a game of hopscotch.

Hopscotch games come in all shapes and sizes. Some have 8 squares in a straight line. Others have as many as 20 squares in the shape of a snail's shell.

Hopscotch is a popular sidewalk game all over the world.

80

Outside a monastery in India, children play hopscotch together.

WORLD BOOK'S CHILDCRAFT

WHO WE ARE

Wonders of Long Ago

Did you know that there are monuments, tombs, and huge walls that were built hundreds or even thousands of years ago? Sometimes only small parts, or ruins, of these places remain. But you can still visit them today.

In England, tourists and scientists alike are amazed by Stonehenge, a group of huge, rough-cut stones set in circles. Scientists believe that ancient people built Stonehenge as a gathering place. Much of the monument is gone, but scientists think that when it was first built, an earth wall about 320 feet (98 meters) across circled it. Thirty blocks of gray sandstone stood like guards 13 1/2 feet (4 meters) above the ground.

Ancient peoples built Stonehenge, in England, more than 3,500 years ago.

Another wonder from long ago is the Great Pyramid at Giza in Egypt. Pyramids were built by Egyptians about 4,500 years ago as tombs for their kings. The Great Pyramid contains more than 2 million stone blocks.

The pyramids of Egypt at Giza were one of the Seven Wonders of the Ancient World.

102   103

Volume 13 *See the World*

Preschool

Activity 1. Volume 13, *See the World,* introduces places of historic significance and natural beauty. Since young children have little sense of the past or of faraway places, try to introduce the book with places that exist now, without emphasizing their location. Read about a place of interest with your child and talk about the picture(s).

Activity 2. Bring out similarities and differences between a place in the book and a place that is familiar to your child. For example, if a picture shows a cathedral, compare it to a place of worship near your home or one that you have visited together. If some of the stories you and your child have read are set in places mentioned in the text, look at the picture together to find things the stories mentioned.

School Age

Activity 1. Explain that the book is organized by themes. Read several titles from the table of contents and invite your child to choose a part in which he or she is interested. Look through the pages together, reading the titles and captions. Encourage your child to look at other parts of the book independently.

Activity 2. Show your child the index of *See the World* and explain the purpose of an index. Ask your child to name different kinds of places, such as a river, castle, or mountain. If those places are listed, look up and read about them with your child.

Volume 14 *Celebrate!*

Preschool

Activity 1. Use a home calendar to introduce Volume 14, *Celebrate!* Explain that this book is about the days of the year and what makes them special. Point out today's date on your home calendar, and turn to the chapter about the month. Compare the two calendars. Explain that the one in the book shows birthdays of famous people. Find today's date and read the name(s). Next, find the calendar in the book that lists your child's birthday. Read the names of famous people with the same birthday.

Activity 2. When your family observes a holiday, look at its text and pictures with your child. For birthdays, use the calendar to learn which famous people share the same birthday.

School Age

Activity 1. Introduce *Celebrate!* by explaining its organization according to the months of the year. Then choose one month—the one with your child's birthday or another month with special significance—and look at the calendar and read one or more articles. Encourage your child to look at the book each month to find some special days.

Activity 2. You can show a child who is reading fairly independently how to use *Celebrate!* for reference. After looking at the month-by-month organization, turn to the index. Read through some of the topics and turn to the pages listed. Help your child see that he or she can use both the table of contents and the index to find information about a date, ceremony, or event.

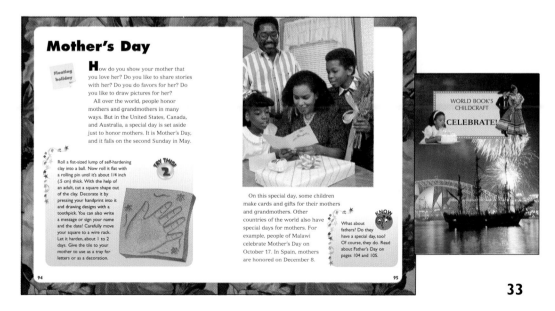

Curriculum Enrichment

The following sections relate *Childcraft* to typical preschool and primary curriculum objectives in eight subject areas: (1) Language and Literature; (2) Critical Thinking Skills; (3) Mathematics; (4) Science; (5) Social Studies; (6) Creative Arts; (7) Self-Understanding, Health, and Safety; and (8) Careers. Each section includes suggested introductory activities.

For additional topics, look in the index at the back of this book.

Language and Literature

Listening

For information. (Primary) Read a short factual article about an animal or animal behaviour (Volume 4), plant life (Volume 5), or a holiday (Volume 14). Then ask several questions that require children to recall details in the article.

For pleasure. (Primary) Read a story in Volume 2 and get children to draw, colour, or paint illustrations of the characters or events in the story.

Speaking

In discussions. (Primary) Read a selection from Volume 12 that discusses a custom or way of life of a different country. Ask the children to describe how this behaviour is like or different from what is done in their own cultures.

Making presentations. (Primary) Challenge a child to read one of the maths puzzles or games in Volume 10. Invite him or her to present the puzzle to other children and, if the other children cannot work it out, to explain the answer or "trick" involved.

Poetry and choral reading. (Preschool) Teach one or more poems in Volume 1 to the children until they can say the poem(s) in unison. Encourage good pronunciation and appropriate expression.

(Primary) Invite the children to choose favourite poems from Volume 1 and read them to the group. As needed, help individual children to select poems at their reading level or prepare the poem for presentation.

What Happens Where You Live?

Neighbors keep things lively in every kind of neighborhood. What do your neighbors do?

These Indian women from Guatemala in Central America weave beautiful rugs and carpets.

These girls pick tea leaves in northeast India.

Many people in Newfoundland live near the ocean and fish for a living.

Dramatics. (Primary) After the children have read or heard one of the stories in Volume 2, ask them to break into small groups to act out the story in front of the class.

Vocabulary

Recognizing context clues. (Primary) When you are reading a passage that explains a new term in context or with the help of an illustration, point out the new term. Reread the passage and encourage the children to raise their hands when they hear its meaning explained.

Using the glossary. (Primary) Distribute Volumes 3–14 to children. Ask them to turn to the glossaries of their volumes. Explain that the glossary for each book is like a dictionary for words that are especially important in that book. Get the children to compare words listed in different volumes.

Writing

Mechanics (prose and poetry). (Primary) Use selections in *Poems and Rhymes* (Volume 1) and *Once Upon a Time* (Volume 2) to point out differences in poetry and stories, such as the use of lines or paragraphs, the use of capital letters, and the length.

Creative writing. (Primary) Read stories to the children from *Once Upon a Time*. Ask the children to write stories of their own.

Report writing. (Primary) Use articles in Volumes 3–14 as models of nonfiction writing. For example, read "Feathers and Wings" (Volume 4, pages 56–57) and ask such questions as "What does the first paragraph tell you?" "How do the next paragraphs help you understand the first paragraph?" and "Is there any other information you need to understand this?"

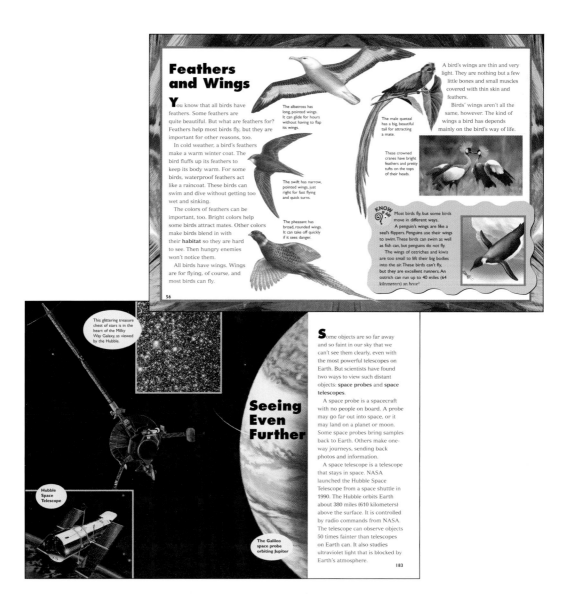

Feathers and Wings

You know that all birds have feathers. Some feathers are quite beautiful. But what are feathers for? Feathers help most birds fly, but they are important for other reasons, too.

In cold weather, a bird's feathers make a warm winter coat. The bird fluffs up its feathers to keep its body warm. For some birds, waterproof feathers act like a raincoat. These birds can swim and dive without getting too wet and sinking.

The colors of feathers can be important, too. Bright colors help some birds attract mates. Other colors make birds blend in with their **habitat** so they are hard to see. Then hungry enemies won't notice them.

All birds have wings. Wings are for flying, of course, and most birds can fly.

56

The albatross has long, pointed wings. It can glide for hours without having to flap its wings.

The swift has narrow, pointed wings, just right for fast flying and quick turns.

The pheasant has broad, rounded wings. It can take off quickly if it sees danger.

A bird's wings are thin and very light. They are nothing but a few little bones and small muscles covered with thin skin and feathers.

Birds' wings aren't all the same, however. The kind of wings a bird has depends mainly on the bird's way of life.

The male quetzal has a big, beautiful tail for attracting a mate.

These crowned cranes have bright feathers and pretty tufts on the tops of their heads.

KNOW 2 Most birds fly, but some birds move in different ways.

A penguin's wings are like a seal's flippers. Penguins use their wings to swim. These birds can swim as well as fish can, but penguins do not fly.

The wings of ostriches and kiwis are too small to lift their big bodies into the air. These birds can't fly, but they are excellent runners. An ostrich can run up to 40 miles (64 kilometers) an hour?

Seeing Even Further

Some objects are so far away and so faint in our sky that we can't see them clearly, even with the most powerful telescopes on Earth. But scientists have found two ways to view such distant objects: **space probes** and **space telescopes**.

A space probe is a spacecraft with no people on board. A probe may go far out into space, or it may land on a planet or moon. Some space probes bring samples back to Earth. Others make one-way journeys, sending back photos and information.

A space telescope is a telescope that stays in space. NASA launched the Hubble Space Telescope from a space shuttle in 1990. The Hubble orbits Earth about 380 miles (610 kilometers) above the surface. It is controlled by radio commands from NASA. The telescope can observe objects 50 times fainter than telescopes on Earth can. It also studies ultraviolet light that is blocked by Earth's atmosphere.

183

This glittering treasure chest of stars is in the heart of the Milky Way Galaxy, as viewed by the Hubble.

Hubble Space Telescope

The Galileo space probe orbiting Jupiter

Reading

Reading readiness. (Preschool) Reinforce your teaching of rhyming sounds by reading some rhymes in Volume 1. Read each poem up to the concluding rhyme, and let the children provide the last word.

Reading in content areas. (Primary) Encourage children to read selections in Volumes 3 to 14 for information and to use their findings in making oral or written reports, posters, or art projects.

Reading techniques—using illustrations. (Preschool, Primary) Encourage children to look through Volumes 3 to 14 for the information they can glean from pictures. Get the children to talk in detail about the pictures they have examined.

Reading techniques—using titles and captions.

(Primary) Ask questions about a selection whose answers can be found in the title or picture caption(s). Allow children a short time to find the answers, and let them tell what led them to a particular answer.

Literature appreciation

Awareness of style and word choice in poetry or prose.

(Primary) Use poems in Volume 1 to compare and contrast two types of writing or writing styles. For example, read Lilian Moore's "Snowy Morning" (page 38), "Thaw" by Eunice Tietjens (page 38), and "Cynthia in the Snow" by Gwendolyn Brooks (page 39). Ask about the different ways the poets describe snow. Ask the children to describe it in their own words.

(Primary) After children have read or heard a selection from *Childcraft*, discuss the words the author uses and their connotations. For example, in "Why Bear Has a Stumpy Tail" (Volume 2, pages 106–107), the fox is described as "slinking along". Ask children whether they think "slinking" is a good descriptive word and how it makes them feel about the fox when they hear it. Ask children to think of other words that might be used in place of "slinking".

Critical Thinking Skills

Classification

(Primary) Read titles of the volumes with the children. Invite them to tell what kinds of things they might read about in each one.

(Primary) Ask children to look at the tables of contents of different volumes and discuss how the topics are grouped in each one.

Drawing comparisons and contrasts

(Primary) Help children use articles about animals and plants in volumes 4 and 5 to discover characteristics of specific types and differences between types. Read the articles to the class, or ask children to read them, and then discuss the information. Get small groups of children to collect magazine and newspaper photographs illustrating some characteristics of a certain group of animals or plants, or have them make charts showing differences between groups.

Separating fact from opinion

(Primary) Read a legend or myth about nature, such as "Myths About the Moon" (Volume 7, pages 42–45), and a factual explanation, "What Is the Moon Like?" (Volume 7, pages 54–55). Then ask children to list the facts about the moon and the ideas people have had about the moon in two separate columns on a paper chart or the board.

Logical reasoning

(Primary) Challenge children to try some activities and puzzles in Volume 10 that require reasoning, such as classifying objects (pages 76–77, 78–79). Ask them to suggest some categories of objects they can use for a scavenger hunt inside or outdoors.

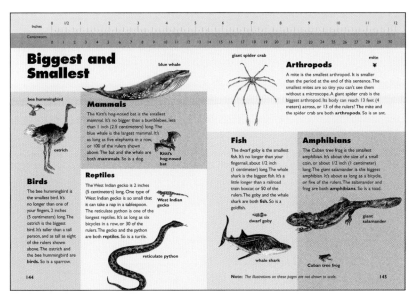

Mathematics

Numbers and numerals

(Primary) Read articles from "The Story of Numbers" in Volume 10, such as pages 46–47, 48–49, and 50–51. Then invite children to count small objects, such as beads or buttons, as described on pages 50–51 and use markers or make marks on paper for each group of 10.

(Primary) Read the articles about numerals and number systems in Volume 10. Then get the children to form groups, and have each group show how numbers would be written in a specific numeral system.

Computing

(Primary) Use articles from "Making Numbers Count," such as "Patterns in Addition," "You Can Add," and "You Can Subtract," to extend your teaching of addition and subtraction. For children who enjoy challenges, use number puzzles such as "Backward Puzzles" and "The Minus Mystery".

Chance

(Primary) Read the article "Sharing Birthdays" on pages 136–137 to children. Ask children to write their names and birthdates (month and day) on slips of paper and compare them to see if any two birthdates are the same.

(Primary) Invite children to test their chances using the two boxes described in "Ali Kwazoor's Choice" on pages 138–141 and the activity on pages 142–143. Get two children to keep score, and let the group take turns picking a stone from each of the two boxes. Total the number for each box to see which box gave them a better chance to pick a black stone.

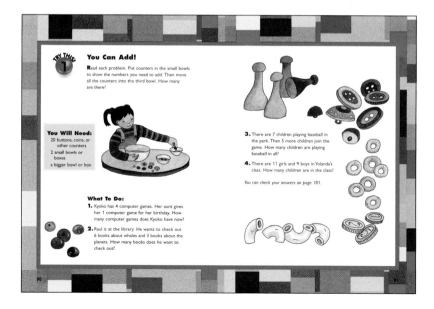

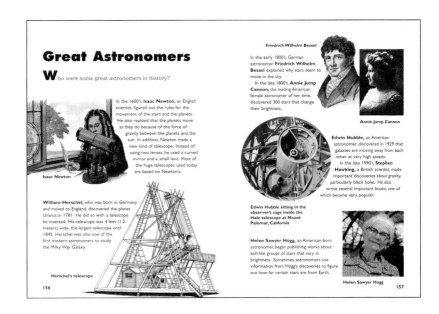

Great Astronomers

Who were some great astronomers in history?

In the 1600's, **Isaac Newton**, an English scientist, figured out the rules for the movement of the stars and the planets. He also realized that the planets move as they do because of the force of gravity between the planets and the sun. In addition, Newton made a new kind of telescope. Instead of using two lenses, he used a curved mirror and a small lens. Most of the huge telescopes used today are based on Newton's.

Isaac Newton

William Herschel, who was born in Germany and moved to England, discovered the planet Uranus in 1781. He did so with a telescope he invented. His telescope was 4 feet (1.2 meters) wide, the largest telescope until 1845. Herschel was also one of the first modern astronomers to study the Milky Way Galaxy.

Herschel's telescope

Friedrich Wilhelm Bessel

In the early 1800's, German astronomer **Friedrich Wilhelm Bessel** explained why stars seem to move in the sky.

In the late 1800's, **Annie Jump Cannon,** the leading American female astronomer of her time, discovered 300 stars that change their brightness.

Annie Jump Cannon

Edwin Hubble, an American astronomer, discovered in 1929 that galaxies are moving away from each other at very high speeds.

In the late 1990's, **Stephen Hawking,** a British scientist, made important discoveries about gravity, particularly black holes. He also wrote several important books, one of which became very popular.

Edwin Hubble sitting in the observer's cage inside the Hale telescope at Mount Palomar, California

Helen Sawyer Hogg, an American-born astronomer, began publishing works about ball-like groups of stars that vary in brightness. Sometimes, astronomers use information from Hogg's discoveries to figure out how far certain stars are from Earth.

Helen Sawyer Hogg

156

157

Science

Awareness of scientific concerns

(Primary) Teach poems about the weather in Volume 1. You may also want to read the poems about night in Volume 1 to introduce the explanation of day and night in Volume 6.

Experimenting, observing

(Primary) Get younger children to do selected activities in Volume 6 with your guidance. Let older children work in small groups. Help younger children record their findings on the board or a paper chart. Older children can record their own findings on a chart or in notebooks.

Testing hypotheses

(Primary) Read the articles about early explanations of the stars and planets in "Studying the Universe" in Volume 7. Ask children to listen for ideas about the sun, moon, and planets that people today would not agree with. Then read additional articles from the chapter, or ask children to read them independently. Get them to name the inventions and experiments that have changed people's earlier ideas.

(Primary) Read the article "Holmes and the *e*" in Volume 10. Let children form four groups. Each group should make up a simple code and write a short saying in the code. Then get groups to exchange messages and try to work out the codes. When a message has been decoded, let the group tell what it says and how they worked it out.

Many children help cook for their family. This boy in the United States is helping to make strawberry jam.

Families play and explore together in all kinds of ways. Some may visit faraway places. This family is hiking in the mountains in France.

What Families Do Together

Families work, learn, grow, and have fun together—each in its own way. Everywhere in the world, family members love and help one another.

Children in many families care for their younger brothers and sisters. This girl in Turkey is keeping an eye on her little brother.

Many families worship together. These children are taking part in a Shinto (SHIHN toh) religious ceremony in Japan.

Many families work together. They grow crops and take care of their homes. These children of Fiji in the South Pacific are helping at harvest time.

In families, people teach and learn from each other. This boy on Africa's Ivory Coast is getting a drum lesson.

20   21

Social Studies

The Family
(Primary) In Volume 11, read articles about the family. In Volume 12, read selected articles from "Families and Neighbours" and talk with children about the families and activities in the photographs. As a group project, create a bulletin-board display on families using children's own poems, stories, and illustrations.

Geography
(Primary) Use Chapter 1 of Volume 13 to develop awareness of oceans and continents. Help children locate them on a world map or globe. As they read other selections, get them to find the places they read about. For example, in Volume 14, they could locate countries that celebrate a holiday.

The Community
(Primary) Enrich studies of housing, food, transportation, or communication by reading aloud or getting children to read selections in Volume 12. Ask children to make collages or give presentations on these themes, using photographs, drawings, music, or plays that illustrate examples from around the world.

Community helpers
(Primary) Read articles in Volume 12 about how people in communities get along. Get children to plan a project to show how helpers in their own community work together. For example, they could make posters or models of doctors, nurses, police officers, rubbish collectors, and other workers and explain their jobs.

Creative Arts

Music

(Primary) Get children to make the rhythm and wind instruments shown in Volume 3. Let them use the instruments to accompany singing or to play melodies and rhythms that they make up.

Sculpture

(Primary) Let children try out basic clay techniques in Volume 3 and create real or fanciful animals. Then let them try the activity that uses "found" household objects to make decorative sculptures called assemblages. Older children will enjoy making the owl piñata for a special occasion.

Painting

(Primary) Use the colour-mixing activity in Volume 3 to help children learn primary and secondary colours. Get them to use the colours to paint with brushes, or let them try out the string-painting activity to experiment with designs.

(Primary) Get children to make the paint described in Volume 3 and use it to paint posters or a wall mural for a science or social studies project.

Theatre

(Primary) Let children form groups and choose stories from Volume 2. Then get them to dramatize it either by taking parts themselves or by making glove puppets or shadow puppets following the Try This! activities from "Theatre Around the World" in Volume 3.

(Primary) Let children act out the African folk tale from "Theatre" in Volume 3, using simple props. Costumes for younger children can be simplified by making only the paper-bag masks described in the Try This! activity that follows the play.

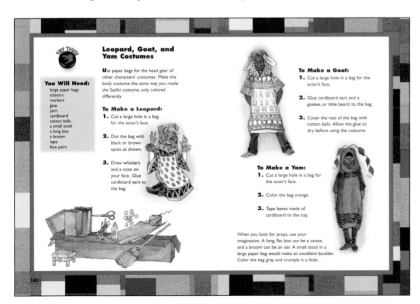

TRY THIS!

Leopard, Goat, and Yam Costumes

Use paper bags for the head gear of other characters' costumes. Make the body costume the same way you made the Sadiki costume, only colored differently.

You Will Need:
large paper bags
scissors
markers
glue
yarn
cardboard
cotton balls
a small stool
a long box
a broom
tape
face paint

To Make a Leopard:
1. Cut a large hole in a bag for the actor's face.
2. Dot the bag with black or brown spots as shown.
3. Draw whiskers and a nose on your face. Glue cardboard ears to the bag.

To Make a Goat:
1. Cut a large hole in a bag for the actor's face.
2. Glue cardboard ears and a goatee, or little beard, to the bag.
3. Cover the rest of the bag with cotton balls. Allow the glue to dry before using the costume.

To Make a Yam:
1. Cut a large hole in a bag for the actor's face.
2. Color the bag orange.
3. Tape leaves made of cardboard to the top.

When you look for props, use your imagination. A long, flat box can be a canoe, and a broom can be an oar. A small stool in a large paper bag would make an excellent boulder. Color the bag gray and crumple it a little.

160

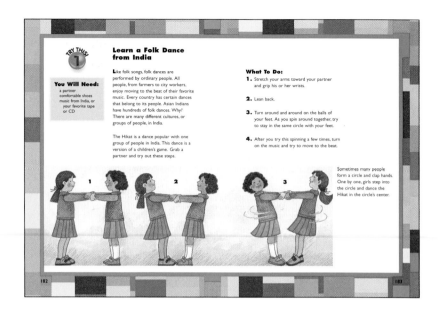

Self-Understanding, Health, and Safety

Games

(Primary) *Childcraft* contains a variety of games and exercises that provide whole-body movement. Let children try the folk dance of India from "Theatre" in Volume 3 and the tag and running games from "What Games Do We Play?" in Volume 12.

Behaviour, Manners, and Attitudes

(Primary) Read and talk about selected articles from "How Do We All Get Along?" in Volume 12. Encourage children to develop projects from their discussions, such as making posters about school rules, performing sketches about good and bad manners, and creating a bulletin board or notebook of stories and pictures about how people in their families help out at home.

Understanding the Body

(Primary) Encourage children to use Volume 11 as a reference book to help them understand how their bodies function and grow.

Careers

(Primary) Get children to look through Volume 12 for photographs and illustrations of people at work. Ask them to tell which ones are like the kinds of work people do in their community. Invite a member of the community who provides a service, such as a police officer, nurse, firefighter, cook, or a supermarket manager, to talk to the class. Or, arrange a short trip to a supermarket, bakery, fire station, library, or other location to see where people work and what they do.

(Primary) Read "People Who Work with Animals" in Volume 4 and let children talk about the kinds of work that interest them. Invite a worker in your community, such as a vet, animal shelter worker, or ranger, to speak to the children.

Work with the children as one group or smaller groups to write a letter of invitation and to think of questions to ask. Check with the person you plan to invite ahead of time to be sure he or she is willing and is available for a group visit.

(Primary) Read to children, or get children to read, some of the articles that introduce people who work in different areas, such as "People Who Work with Animals" in Volume 4, "Taking Care of Forests" in Volume 5, and "Keeping Track" in Volume 6. Encourage children to look through *Childcraft* for other kinds of jobs that interest them and collect magazine and newspaper pictures, articles, and material from the school library or the Internet about the career topics they choose.

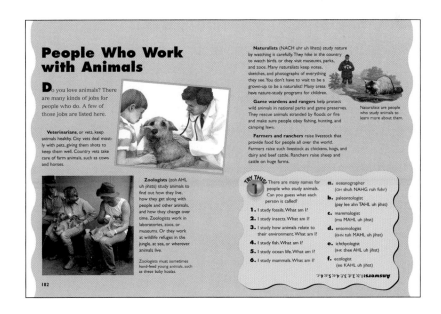

People Who Work with Animals

Do you love animals? There are many kinds of jobs for people who do. A few of those jobs are listed here.

Veterinarians, or vets, keep animals healthy. City vets deal mostly with pets, giving them shots to keep them well. Country vets take care of farm animals, such as cows and horses.

Zoologists (zoh AHL uh jihsts) study animals to find out how they live, how they get along with people and other animals, and how they change over time. Zoologists work in laboratories, zoos, or museums. Or they work at wildlife refuges in the jungle, at sea, or wherever animals live.

Zoologists must sometimes hand-feed young animals, such as these baby koalas.

Naturalists (NACH uhr uh lihsts) study nature by watching it carefully. They hike in the country to watch birds, and they visit museums, parks, and zoos. Many naturalists keep notes, sketches, and photographs of everything they see. You don't have to wait to be a grown-up to be a naturalist! Many areas have nature-study programs for children.

Game wardens and rangers help protect wild animals in national parks and game preserves. They rescue animals stranded by floods or fire and make sure people obey fishing, hunting, and camping laws.

Farmers and ranchers raise livestock that provide food for people all over the world. Farmers raise such livestock as chickens, hogs, and dairy and beef cattle. Ranchers raise sheep and cattle on huge farms.

Naturalists are people who study animals to learn more about them.

TRY THIS 1 There are many names for people who study animals. Can you guess what each person is called?

1. I study fossils. What am I?
2. I study insects. What am I?
3. I study how animals relate to their environment. What am I?
4. I study fish. What am I?
5. I study ocean life. What am I?
6. I study mammals. What am I?

a. oceanographer (OH shuh NAHG ruh fuhr)
b. paleontologist (pay lee ahn TAHL uh jihst)
c. mammalogist (ma MAHL uh jihst)
d. entomologist (EHN tuh MAHL uh jihst)
e. ichthyologist (IHK thee AHL uh jihst)
f. ecologist (ee KAHL uh jihst)

Answers: 1.b; 2.d; 3.f; 4.e; 5.a; 6.c.

182

Growth and Development

The preschool years, from about age 3 to 5, are truly formative years, marked by intellectual growth, rapidly developing motor skills, increasing social maturity, and emotional richness. Preschool children are eager to learn and excited about the world. Children between 5 and 8 years old are alert, high-spirited, and full of ideas and questions. Their first years in school are some of the most crucial years of their education, a time when a solid foundation for learning and positive self-esteem are formed. Parents and teachers play an essential role during these years—guiding, reassuring, teaching, and loving children so that they get the best possible start in their lives.

Preschool Children: 3 to 5 years

The way children use tricycles says a lot about how their motor skills are developing. At 3, they almost surely enjoy riding on trikes. At first, they may be content to sit on the seat. Then they start to use the pedals but don't quite get the hang of them. Sometimes they want to move forwards, but the trike goes backwards. When they master the basics, they ride along deliberately for a while, proud of their new skills. Soon they discover how far they can go. They don't slow down for turns. They ride as close to people as they can. If they have to stop, they wait until the last second and then come to a fast, hard stop.

Parents also see progress in motor development as children acquire skill in dressing. By the time they are 3, children can unbutton their clothes, but they have a hard time buttoning them. They cannot tell the back from the front, so they often put trousers on backwards. They may still need help in putting on shirts, sweaters, and other clothes. When they are 4, children can dress with little help, although the process may seem to take forever.

The Preschool Child's Development

Social development

The way two preschool children play together on their tricycles shows changes in social growth as well as motor development. Three-year-olds may simply like to be near each other on their trikes. They may bump each other experimentally. A bit of giggling often goes along with the bumps, but there is seldom much conversation. One child may decide to wander off somewhere nearby—at this age, children do not yet go far afield. Another child will probably follow, but not always right away. The social response is not yet quick, sure, and certain.

As they near their fifth birthdays, children are very different. There is almost no sitting still. They are sure to be on the go. Now the children play together. They have plans and they talk about them, sometimes with a few arguments. Once they think up an idea, each one is likely to carry it out with modifications that make the plan his or her own. They have grown into social creatures who get thrills from being with each other.

The pleasure of each other's company and the excitement of doing things together sometimes become so overwhelming that toilet-trained children forget to use the toilet. In their own list of priorities, these preschool children have put first things first. To them, playing with a friend is more important.

Language development

Another major advance of these years, along with social development, is the development of language. By the time children are about 4, they can be chatterboxes.

Preschool children do not simply chatter, however. Their language involves all the parts of speech, longer sentences, and greater clarity. Language development and social development aid one another. Most preschool children still fight at times. However, they gradually learn to settle disputes with words.

This tremendous growth in speech can be exasperating to adults. The children seem to talk too much. They frequently interrupt because what they have to say is the most important thing in the world to them. They often talk too loudly. Around age 4, it is common for them to go on a spree of name-calling and experimenting with non-sensical singsongs.

One other characteristic is their never-ending questions. Inquiries increase and become more complex from about 3 years on. "How?" and "Why?" questions continue as children try to understand relationships, how things work, and what they are for.

Preschool Education

Preschool children's constant questions reflect another side of their development in these years—their intense curiosity and thirst for knowledge. One of their most outstanding characteristics is that they are so completely ready to learn about the world around them, about themselves as a part of that world, about other children, and about adults. Preschool children are curious, open, and responsive. Their eyes go out to all that is around them. Their hands are tools for exploration.

One of the most important tasks for parents is to keep this burning curiosity and charmed sense of wonder alive. Most parents appreciate curiosity. Sometimes, however, they unintentionally discourage it. Children's curiosity may sometimes be troubling and frightening. Parents worry about safety, so they sometimes curtail children's activities to keep them safe. However, when parents' irritations or worries mount, children may hear "No," "Don't," "Be careful," and "Watch out" too often. Parents must take precautions, of course. But at the same time, they need to avoid giving the message that the world is a bad or dangerous place.

By stimulating children's curiosity, parents help them reach their creative potential. Most important, by nurturing children's curiosity, parents help set them on course for a richer, more fulfilling life.

Taking day trips

Day trips are one of the best ways to bring stimulating experiences to young children. They are basically uninformed—they simply do not

A shopping trip is an adventure.

know much yet because they have not experienced much. No one can tell children at this age about the world. They have to see and experience things firsthand, so day trips are perfect learning opportunities.

Day trips for preschool children should be short. Young children tire easily, and tired, irritable children learn very little. The destination does not have to be spectacular. To young children, the supermarket, post office, park, and other every-day locations are a treat.

A good day trip is one that has a slow, relaxed pace with time for talking. There also ought to be time for several short stops along the way. And on any journey, children need time to stand and watch, to touch, and to explore. They cannot take in all they want to know at a glance. On trips, there are countless opportunities to point out sights children might otherwise miss. In addition, there are many opportunities for children to ask questions that might not otherwise occur to them.

Reading stories

Good storybooks, like good trips, stimulate children. Stories bring a part of the world closer to them so that they can take a closer look at it and come to understand it more fully. Stories may be make-believe or about real people or events. They may involve animals that seem almost human. They may include

Reading stories out loud gives children a chance to ask questions and learn.

more adventure than most people have in their everyday lives. But fiction or nonfiction, children's books help children to learn more about the people, events, and objects in their environment.

The trick in reading stories to children is the same as the key to taking successful day trips. Take your time. Do not rush to the end of the story. Let children interrupt to ask questions. Story time should

A large cardboard box—one that the child can't close completely—can stimulate highly imaginative play.

be a daily event—a time for companionship and conversation.

Enriching play

To adults looking on, preschool children seem to spend all of their time just playing. This play is far from a waste of time, however. It is a highly significant activity that teaches important emotional, intellectual, and social lessons.

Children at play draw on what they know. They often play house, for example, mostly because life at home is what they know best. The play is imaginative, but it is firmly grounded in reality. The more children know—the more places they have been, the more things they have seen—the richer their play will be. Preschool children also need toys and other materials with which to carry out their play. The same toys should be for all to use. Girls may want to play with trains, and boys may want to play house with toy plates. Nothing should be specifically earmarked for boys or for girls.

Good preschool toys set up rough outlines and give children's fertile minds freedom to fill in the details. A tricycle, for example, is obviously some kind of moving vehicle, but children decide whether it is a horse, ambulance, or rocket. Among the best playthings are boards, boxes, blankets, sand, bricks, cartons, wagons, chairs, dolls, simple cars and boats, and other materials that can be used in various ways.

Growing language and social development, increased knowledge, longer attention span, and vastly improved physical co-ordination all combine to produce the most distinctive characteristic of preschool children: their capacity for make-believe. Children can take on any role that suits their fancy. They can be cowboys, princesses, or tigers. A chair can become a horse, plane, or animal cage.

One kind of imaginative activity special to this age is playing with an imaginary playmate. Imaginary playmates may be someone to boss around or someone who gives support and comfort. These unseen friends can be important to some children. If children begin mentioning some unseen friend, adults should play along. This will give children confidence in the real friends they have in the adults around them.

Television viewing and preschool children

The fascination television holds for young children is an indication of their thirst for stimulation. TV's fast-moving pictures and continuous sound lure many young children into watching contentedly for hours. For better or for worse, television is a teacher. Television viewing affects children's language and their awareness of the world around them.

Television also provides relaxation and entertainment. However, TV viewing can present hazards. There is reason to worry about the impact of TV's violence on the feelings and morals of children, about the impact of commercials on their taste, and about the effect of long hours of passive watching on their personalities. Parents also must be concerned because too much TV viewing can rob a family of time for talk and shared activities, and also can deprive children of creative play with friends. These hazards increase if the TV is allowed to become a babysitter.

Some families react to these concerns by having no TV set. However, when TV is available, it is important for parents to make thoughtful decisions about what programmes their children may watch and how long they may watch. Involving preschool children in these decisions offers them learning experiences about choices and responsibilities.

It also is wise for parents to watch television with their children often enough to discuss with them the ideas, feelings, and values the programmes generate. If good programmes are available, and if viewing hours are wisely regulated,

Young children happily watch TV. They need help in choosing and setting limits.

television can be a positive educational force. For additional information, see "Children, Television, and the Internet" on page 94.

Sending preschool children to school

Many 3- and 4-year-olds go to preschools, also known as nursery schools, playgroups, or kindergartens. Some are in preschool because their parents want to supplement the stimulation and companionship they can offer at home. Others are in preschool because one or both parents work, and the children need day care. See the article "Choosing Day Care" on page 91.

The organization of preschools differs from country to country and from area to area. Some are parent-co-operative schools, which are owned and operated by parents. The parents hire a teacher and take turns helping out in the classroom and doing the other work of the school. Some preschools are operated by community or religious groups. Others are run by individuals, corporations, or state-school systems.

At preschool, children move about the room a lot. They begin to learn to live, work, and play together. They learn to take turns, settle disputes fairly, and co-operate. They hear stories and music. They may take short educational trips. They also have the opportunity to express themselves through playthings and artwork. A good preschool has both indoor and outdoor facilities and gives ample time for climbing, balancing, swinging, and other activities that build muscle co-ordination. Preschool children are almost constantly involved in make-believe play, which gives them the chance to use their initiative, think, plan, develop their attention spans, and build their capacity for problem solving.

Through all these activities, preschools aim to develop in children the habits, attitudes, and skills that will help them in school. Preschools also help children develop their intellectual and physical skills. Preschools aid in the development of good health and safety habits and encourage independence.

Preschool is not for everyone, however. Some children have trouble adjusting to preschool, especially if they've never spent much time away from their parents. Preschool also may be too demanding and stressful for some children. Another downside to preschools is that they can expose children to more viruses, resulting in more illness.

Common Preschool Concerns

The preschool period can be a happy time in family life, free from overwhelming problems. One reason is that preschool children can do so much more for themselves. They can be independent in feeding themselves, dressing, and using the toilet. They no longer place the constant physical demands on their parents that they did as infants. Another reason is that they delight in the world and in the people around them. Their eagerness, openness, and good feelings about being alive can be quite contagious. No age, however, is completely angelic. There are always some rough spots.

Dealing with dawdling

The conflict between young children's time schedules and that of their parents is often a trouble area. Most adults watch the time. They are going somewhere and know exactly how many minutes they need to get there. Young children often stop and watch the world go by. Adults call this action "dawdling". For children, of course, this is simply the way they act. It is a part of the newness of being able to do things for one's self.

The best approach for coping with dawdling is to make some minor adjustments. For example, with eating and dressing, parents should allow as much time as possible so that children can move at their own pace. But if something pressing lies ahead, parents should pitch in with a helping hand to speed up the eating or dressing process. They should not nag or pester. Angry words seldom produce a speed-up. There will be times when reality demands that the meal be ended—for example, when the available time has simply run out. There is no great harm in children experiencing this. In fact, they begin to learn that time has limits. The harm comes only when, as the food is taken away, adult anger, nagging, and complaining come to take its place.

Understanding fears

Some problems arise, too, because it is so easy to forget that 3-year-olds in particular, but also 4-year-olds, are still little, dependent children. When parents forget this, they often are harsher than they should be. This is especially true when these children get frightened. And a wide, unpredictable range of events and sounds and sights can scare them.

The quick, easy response to children's fear is the pep talk: "You're not afraid of a little thing like that, are you?" The only reply, which is often screamed with the whole body, is to say in effect, "I certainly am afraid . . . that's what this fuss is all about". Worse than the pep talk is unsympathetic scoffing and shaming: "Don't be silly . . . . Don't be a cry-baby". When children are afraid of dogs, thunder, or the dark, it hardly helps to have the added fear of losing their parents' love and respect.

An effective first step in dealing with fright is to accept it. Parents should give support and comfort so that frightened children feel strong enough to face the frightening event. Parents can acknowledge fear in supportive ways, such as saying, "All that noise does seem a little scary," while reassuring them that they are not in danger. Sometimes just moving over to be close is all the support that is needed. Children who are deeply upset have to be held, patted, and comforted. The goal is to give enough support so that they feel better, without protecting them so much that they feel pushed back into babyhood. When frightened children have calmed down a bit, parents can try to teach them how to cope with the experience the next time it happens. The more competence children have, the fewer fears there will be.

The most upsetting fear of all occurs when children think their parents do not love them. Any one of a wide variety of events can start this unhappy train of thought. Separation is a problem. When young children are left alone in a strange new setting such as a hospital, a doctor's surgery, or preschool, they can easily translate "Separation—they are leaving me" into "Separation—they don't love me". Harshness, coldness, and busyness can have the same effect. Children in these situations can feel alone and unprotected.

Sometimes events that parents think ought to make children feel grown-up have the opposite effect, and children become fearful. Getting accustomed to a new baby in the family and starting school are two events that parents often think will make children feel more mature but often stimulate fear instead. In such situations, it is best for parents to be understanding until children are able to adjust to the new situation and overcome any fears.

Developing discipline

Developing good discipline in children is one of the most important jobs of parenthood. But this vital task takes time, patience, and understanding.

Many parents believe that children resent discipline. These parents not only hesitate to punish their children but also seldom use effective ways of building discipline. They want to be good to their children and end up being too lenient. Undisciplined children never know the limits of acceptable behaviour, and this is very unsettling for them. They need someone to teach them what is right or wrong, and why.

Getting a child's attention is a first step in explaining the rules and teaching appropriate behaviour.

Wise parents do not shrink from disciplining their children. They try to work out why their children misbehave and then take whatever action best fits the situation. For example, young children often misbehave because they simply do not know any better. When this is the problem, one appropriate method of discipline is patiently to explain what the rules are and why rules are important. The goal is to teach so that children will understand.

Teaching as a method of discipline is effective only if parents believe in what they are saying, however. They must convey to children that the lesson is important. They must take time to make sure that the child is paying attention and not simply listening with only half an ear. When a parent says, "Stop," and explains why, the child's action must stop— at least for that moment.

Reasoning is an effective but slow method of discipline. It is slow because children cannot be expected to learn after discussing an incident just once. They must hear the lesson over and over again. But in the long run, reasoning is a good method because it helps children learn values that they can use as they grow and mature. It is also a method that respects children's growing independence.

Besides teaching and reasoning, using praise is one of the best ways to encourage good behaviour, especially when it directly follows good behaviour. For example, if children come to the table with clean hands, or act in a way that is expected, immediate praise should be offered. Welcome approval reinforces children's good behaviour, making it more likely to be repeated.

"Not knowing any better" is only one reason for misbehaviour. At times, children do the wrong thing because of what is going on around them. When this seems to be the case, the way to discipline is not through discussion but through action. Parents should change the setting to make it easier for children to be good. This approach is especially useful with children too young to understand words, but it also works with older children. For example, things that toddlers should not touch should be put out of reach. Older children who have to sit for a long time will behave much better if they are given a book to read or a game to play.

Some misbehaviour is rooted in children's feelings. Children have to feel right to act right. Some children are driven to misbehaviour because they desperately need more love, more attention, or a feeling of importance. They do things they know they should not do. A jealous child, for example, may hurt a baby sister or brother. The temptation is to punish children driven by upset feelings, but the surest way to help them is to give them the love or attention or importance their behaviour shows they need.

Parents have to be thoughtful in choosing an approach to discipline. They need to pick the one that fits each child and each situation. This sensitive process of deciding what action to take itself contributes to discipline. It is an expression of love, and the foundation of all good behaviour is children's sense of being loved. Children unconsciously identify with parents who show their love. Slowly but steadily, they will take on the attitudes and values of their parents. What is learned through this process of identification does not reveal itself immediately, but the lessons are instilled in children. Good behaviour will evolve in time.

Health and Safety of Preschool Children

For information on growth, see "Following the Growth of Young Children" on page 85.

Dental care

Regular dental examinations are the surest way for children to enjoy healthy teeth that will last a lifetime. Children's first visit to the dentist should be made at the age of 3, soon after all the primary teeth have appeared. Before their first visit, children should accompany a parent on a routine dental visit. Most dentists will allow children to sit in the dentist's chair, examine some of the instruments, and become acquainted with the dentist and the surroundings. Then the first real visit will not be strange and scary.

At home, parents should encourage children to brush after every meal and snack. Parents should ask the dentist when their children should begin to floss. Parents should allow children to pick out a toothbrush and supply an attractive cup for rinsing the mouth to make brushing more fun.

Good dental care begins with good brushing habits in the early years.

Avoiding accidents

Preschool children are accident-prone. In fact, many children under 4 years old die every month because of serious accidents, most of which can be prevented.

Accidents often happen because parents are not aware of what their children can do. By the time they are at preschool, children can walk, run, climb, jump, and explore everything. Because of all the new things they can do, this stage can be a very dangerous time. It is the parents' responsibility to protect children from injury. Children have a hard time remembering "No" while exploring. In addition, they don't completely understand danger.

Parents should teach children how to recognize and react to dangerous situations and how to develop sound safety habits. In addition, parents should be good role models of safety habits, make rules and enforce them, create a safe environment, and be aware that young children need constant supervision.

Here are some suggestions for teaching safety:

- As situations arise, teach children rules about street and traffic safety, "stranger danger," animal safety, water safety, fire safety, and playground safety. For help, parents can talk to their child's pediatrician and refer to books from bookshops or the library.

- Watch some appropriate television shows with preschool children. This is an excellent way to teach safety by identifying and discussing hazardous and unrealistic situations with them.
- Read age-appropriate books about safety. These are widely available at bookshops or libraries.
- Take children to safety demonstrations sponsored by community agencies such as the local police, fire department, or the Red Cross.
- Make the children active members in "safety surveillance". For example, make children responsible for picking up toys after play and storing them in safe places. Children can tag along on periodic safety checks of the home. This will give them the opportunity to see how smoke alarms work, how the house is made safer for younger siblings, how play areas are checked for safety, and so on. Give children responsibility for reminding others to wear their seat belts in cars and for checking the street for cars before others are allowed to cross.
- Conduct family fire drills. Involve children in the drills and encourage them to ask questions about things they don't understand.

Making the home safe for preschool children is a never-ending task. Their growing abilities and curiosity keep safety-conscious parents constantly on their toes. To begin, parents should get down—literally—to their children's level and take a look around the house from their perspective. This exercise alone points out many of the hazards that lurk about the house, such as furniture with sharp corners protruding at their level or strong cleaning materials within easy reach. Here are a few other tips for creating a safe home environment for preschoolers.

- To avoid falls, use gates on stairways and instal window guards above the first floor.
- Find something safe for children to do while adults are cooking. If children are underfoot, hot liquids, grease, and hot foods can spill and cause serious burns. If children do get burned, immediately run cold water over the burned area. Then cover the burn loosely with a bandage or clean cloth.

- Buy and instal smoke and carbon monoxide detectors. Test their batteries every month to be sure they work. Change the batteries twice a year.
- Set the water temperature in the home to no higher than 50 °C.
- Use only household products and medicines that are absolutely necessary, and keep them safely capped and out of sight and reach. Post the phone number of your doctor near the telephone.
- Lock up or make inaccessible all areas where tools, knives, matches, and other potentially hazardous items are kept.

Above all else, parents' primary responsibility for the safety of preschool children is supervision—both at home and away. Parents should thoroughly investigate the homes of child minders, preschools, and day-care centres. They should choose only those that are safe and have reputable care providers.

Enjoying Your Preschool Child

The preschool years can be a delightful time for families. The children are now beyond the age when they need constant physical care, and they have not yet reached the age when they will be so wrapped up in school demands and friends that parents feel squeezed out of their children's lives. Parents are lucky—and obviously the children are lucky—when whole families can find time to enjoy these years together.

These years are a time for companionship—a time for walks together and short trips. They are a time for shared experiences at home. Children have their moments of wanting to work along with parents, helping in their own way with cooking, cleaning, and other interesting household and garden chores.

These years are a time for words, stories, and music. They are a time for reading together and talking about books. They are the years for listening to children and for talking with children. Children ask all about the ins and outs of their environment and give parents ample opportunity for explaining and interpreting the world. Preschool children's behaviour gives parents many opportunities to talk about values and discipline.

These years are a time for the shared awe and delight in the charming, never-ending variety of our world: insects and nuts and bolts, seashells and cars, snake skins and leaves, the birth of baby kittens, and the screeching of a bright red fire engine.

Parents who work outside the home must make careful plans to find the time to share all this with their children. The special effort it takes proves very rewarding to parents and children alike.

Lucky parents and lucky preschool children enjoy many times together. But wise parents know that even during these early years, children need more people than just their parents. These are wonderful years for children to come to know their wider family of grandparents, uncles, aunts, and cousins. These are the years when parents can help their children find friends in the family doctor and dentist. They are also a good time for children to discover the librarian in the public library.

Equally important, preschool children need friends of their own age. Accommodating children's increasingly strong social drive is one of the values of a good nursery school or playgroup for children whose parents work or who are from one-parent homes. It is also one of the reasons for preschools. Parents also can satisfy their children's need and yearning for companionship

For a preschool child, a grandparent can be a special friend as well as a family member.

through organizing play groups or taking turns with friends and neighbours in watching each other's children. Some parents invite their children's friends to come to the house to play or to join the family on a day trip.

It's easy to overestimate what preschool children can do and expect too much from them. It also is easy to underestimate them and offer too little physical challenge and social and intellectual stimulation. Parents' best safeguard and guide is to keep a watchful eye, judge from children's behaviour how they are feeling at the moment—big and brave and bold, or young and dependent on grown-ups—and enjoy them just the way they are.

School-Age Children: 5 to 8 years

It is easy to see how much 8-year-olds have changed since age 5. It is not so easy to look at 5-year-olds and realize how much they will change in the next 3 years. It is, however, important that parents of children entering school should be able to look ahead. Parents should be aware of the many changes that will occur in their children during the early school years so that they will be better able to meet children's physical, mental, emotional, and social needs.

The School-Age Child's Development

Following social development

At this age, boys mostly play with boys and girls with girls. When no children of the same sex live in the neighbourhood, children usually find playmates in school or through a religious organization, group lessons, sports, or a group with whom the family socializes.

Children between 5 and 8 years have a lot of initiative. They are interested in accomplishments and want to do things well. They need encouragement and respect.

School gives children new opportunities for social development.

School-age children like the feeling of responsibility—of doing something necessary to make the home operate smoothly. Children should be given some responsibilities as part of the household. Tasks should be those that children are capable of handling, such as making their own beds, cleaning their rooms, feeding family pets, setting the table, or putting groceries away.

When children start school, an important person enters their lives—their teacher. The teacher is often the first adult friend that children make on their own. Most children are aware of every detail of their teacher's appearance and respond to every smile or frown. If they like their teacher, they want their parents to feel the same way.

Using parents as role models

Children model themselves largely on their parents. They do so mainly by identifying with a parent. The things parents do and say—and the way they do and say them—will strongly influence children's behaviour. This is why it is important for parents to behave like the type of person they want their children to become.

Parents' actions also affect the self-image that children form through identification. Children who see mainly positive qualities in their parents will likely learn to see themselves in a positive way. Children who observe chiefly negative qualities in their parents will have difficulty seeing positive qualities in themselves. Children may modify their self-image, however, as they become increasingly influenced by peer group standards in later years.

Isolated events, even dramatic ones, do not necessarily have a permanent effect on children's behaviour. Children interpret such events according to how their parents deal with them, their own established attitudes, and their previous training. For example, many children who know they are loved can accept the divorce of their parents or a parent's early death. On the other hand, if children feel unloved, they may interpret such events as a sign of rejection or punishment.

In the same way, children are not equally influenced by toys, books, magazines, television programmes, and Internet activities. The effect of an activity or experience depends on how children interpret it. Children's interpretations, in turn, depend on their standards of behaviour. For instance, violent behaviour on television may heighten the aggressive tendencies of children who consider such behaviour permissible. However, children who have learned that violent behaviour is wrong are less likely to be influenced by TV violence. The day-to-day behaviour and lessons of parents have a more powerful influence on children than do isolated events and experiences.

Making visits away from home

Through visits away from home, school-age children gradually develop social graces and independence. They try out new foods and become accustomed to unfamiliar routines. They learn new skills by sharing family chores in other households. They make friends with children in other communities. Children also develop skills in relating to people away from home. They learn that all families are not alike. Visits to homes of friends for playing, eating a meal, or spending the night all add to their social development.

Before allowing a visit away from home, parents should consider a number of things. For example, does the child really want to spend the night away from home? Is the host family reasonable and flexible? Will they be patient as the child tries to fit into their situation? Have they been told of the child's special needs? Is the child a bed-wetter—a condition that would be acceptable in some households and unacceptable in others? Does the child have occasional nightmares? Is the child allergic to certain foods or materials? Prospective hosts should be told about any special needs of the child before final plans for the

Children can help parents pick out new clothes.

visit are made. This gives them the chance to reconsider if the child's needs seem too great a responsibility for them.

Making choices

During the school-age years, children learn to make choices. And parents can find many ways to give children the opportunity to make them. For example, children may have definite preferences in food and the way food is prepared and served. Some children eat vegetables only if they are raw. Some prefer fruit juice to fresh fruit. So long as the alternatives are convenient and children are eating nutritionally balanced meals, parents should allow children to make food choices. The experience adds to their personal development.

Clothes presents still more opportunities for children to make choices. Parents can allow children to decide what to wear each day.

Children also can help pick out new clothes at the shop. At this age, children may start to be caught up in fads. Sometimes, trainers are the important symbol, and the brand name or label may be as important as the style. Hairstyle, jewellery, the cut of trousers, the type of jacket— all of these things may be driven by popular trends. Again, parents should respect children's choices with regard to their appearance, within reason.

Receiving an allowance

Giving a regular allowance can be a worthwhile educational experience for children. An allowance gives children a realistic, firsthand experience in planning how to spend or save money and how to get full value for it. An allowance also provides children with a natural opportunity to learn arithmetic and to begin to develop a sense of logic.

Children may buy unwisely at first or spend all their money immediately, forgetting that no more will be forthcoming for several days. However, this may help children to learn to choose wisely and spend carefully, because an allowance also involves making choices.

Parents may wish to start with a small weekly allowance and give the same sum on the same day of each week. As children learn the possibilities and limitations of the allowance, and as their needs multiply, the amount can be increased. Children will become ready to take on the additional responsibility of managing the money needed for school expenses—bus fare, school supplies, or lunch money. As the amount of allowance grows, parents may want to discuss how to budget the allowance. They can help children work out how much must be spent each week on essential expenses. Parents also may want to talk about ways of spending or saving any extra money—such as money that they earn doing special chores or receive as gifts.

An allowance should be considered a child's share of the family income and, therefore, should be no more than the family can afford. An allowance should also be considered a child's own money. Parents should allow children to make mistakes and learn from them. Allowances should not be withheld because of disobedience, poor school results, or unwise spending.

An allowance should not be considered a bargaining tool to guarantee children's good behaviour, nor should it be considered a bribe.

Following motor development

"Slow but steady" characterizes the development of motor skills during the school-age years. For example, many 5-year-olds have not yet mastered writing. The small muscles that control fingers and hands are still developing. Writing also requires hand-eye co-ordination, which also is not yet well developed in some 5-year-olds. Even 6-year-olds still find writing difficult.

Seven-year-olds usually concentrate hard when writing. They grip the pencil tightly and usually hold it close to the point. Their letters are uneven in size. By the time they are 8, their hand-eye co-ordination and the small muscles in their hands and fingers are much better developed, and they write more evenly and easily. Physical maturity and better concentration also aid children's writing.

Children's large muscles also are still developing. Girls at this age are better co-ordinated than boys. Both boys and girls are physically active—they run climb, skip, hop, and jump, and they like to be on the go at all times. Too long a time assigned to a chair and desk without a break can lead to restlessness and boredom.

Blocks, paints, and other art activities involve both large-muscle and small-muscle motor skills.

Following other physical characteristics

Growth in height and weight from age 5 to 8 is also slow but steady. The average child adds 5 to 6 centimetres in height and 2 or 3 kilograms in weight each year. For more information, see "Following the Growth of Young Children" on page 85.

A distinguishing characteristic of young school-age children is their smile—and the wide-open spaces that show where primary teeth have fallen out to make room for permanent teeth. At this time, six-year molars are breaking through, and permanent incisors are beginning to appear.

The Early School Years

Starting school

Starting school is a major adventure and a dramatic change for most children. Most of them can hardly wait to start school. They take this challenge in their stride because their normal growth—in language, attention span, social interests, curiosity, and independence—enables them to welcome school without strain. There are, however, a few ways parents can make it even easier for children to begin their school life without emotional upsets.

Adjusting to school will be easier if children have had the experience of being away from home without their parents. Children who have often gone to the shop with a neighbour, eaten lunch at a friend's house, or visited nearby relatives—or who have attended preschool or playgroup— usually have no problems with leaving home and adjusting to the classroom environment.

School adjustment also will be easier for children who have experienced accepting people other than their parents as authorities. Children who have been in the care of good babysitters, for example, will probably have less trouble accepting a teacher. Children who have played with their friends in a neighbourhood garden or a house down the street, responding to whatever adult was in charge of the play, have a good foundation for working with a teacher.

Most children beginning primary school reception classes know other children who will be their classmates. Seeing familiar faces helps children adjust. If children have no friends in school, parents can invite one or two future classmates over to play or for lunch so that there will indeed be one or two familiar faces on the first day of school.

Most schools set aside a day for children to visit their prospective classroom for a short time and meet some of their future classmates. A

Many children are ready and able to leave home and adjust to school.

Seeing familiar faces and finding new friends make the first days of school exciting.

reading and writing, social sciences, mathematics, science, music, and art. Sometimes these subjects are not taught as separate courses. Instead, they may be integrated into a total experience.

Children learn best through firsthand experiences—seeing, hearing, touching, smelling, and above all, doing. Children need these firsthand experiences before they can learn to read. Some children arrive at school able to print, identify letters, or even read a little. Others are unable to do these things. Both are perfectly normal. By the end of first year, most children have learned to associate the sounds in words with written letters, and they are able to spell many words by

few typical activities may be carried out to let children sample what a school day will be like.

Building a foundation for learning

Some school-age children approach learning in a systematic manner. They proceed in logical, methodical ways. Others are cautious. They move forwards only when they are sure of themselves. Still others dive in and then look around. Both parents and teachers must understand and accommodate each child's unique way of learning.

In the early years, children are taught to read, write, and work with numbers. The curriculum includes

Reading, writing, and numbers are basic learning tools.

71

applying simple phonetic rules. Many are reading.

Social studies in these early years generally include learning about people and the world around them. A group of children may study their town and the neighbourhoods and people who make it work. Children are encouraged to discuss their observations and ask questions. What begins as a study of "our community" in the early school years grows into the study of geography, economics, consumer education, ecology, science, safety, history, mapmaking, and map reading in the years to come.

Science is experienced firsthand, too. For example, children may prove that a magnet will only attract things made of iron by conducting experiments with a magnet and various objects. Then children may make magnets. Next, they may make a compass or a buzzer to discover how magnets are used in different objects. By making these items, children begin to understand how they work.

School-age children enjoy music and art. Most of them love to sing, and some even make up their own songs. They use such rhythm instruments as drums, cymbals, and tambourines. They like moving, dancing, and dramatizing or marching to music. Most school-age children like to paint, work with clay, and draw pictures with crayons and pencils.

School-age children also like stories and poetry. They enjoy being read to, an activity that not only stimulates imagination and improves concentration, but also helps strengthen the bond between the teacher and children. When given the opportunity, children compose delightful stories and often write interesting poems.

The monthly calendar is also a learning device. At first, the calendar does not mean much to children. But as days go by, they begin to learn the days of the week, dates in sequence, weekdays and weekend days, and the meaning of time and its components. Children have experiences with words, letters, numbers, holidays, and seasons.

Magnets provide fascinating science experiences for young children.

Meetings give parents and teachers a chance to raise questions, exchange observations, and set goals.

Establishing the home-school relationship

The basis for the home-school relationship forms during the early years of school. Parents should try to meet children's teachers before school starts. At this meeting, parents should talk openly about their children. Then, when school starts, the teacher will already know something about the children and will be able to help each one develop.

Most schools provide time for parent-teacher meetings throughout the school year. Parent-teacher meetings serve both teachers and parents by helping them to identify and discuss the unique needs and interests of each child.

At meetings, teachers can describe their goals for the year, give parents samples of their children's work, and discuss children's behaviour, habits, attitudes, capabilities, strengths, and weaknesses. Meetings give parents a chance to raise questions that cannot be answered adequately by written reports, and they give teachers an opportunity to learn more about the children's lives outside of school. Meetings help parents and teachers work together to help children reach their potential. Parents also may want to meet the parents of other children in the classroom. This will help them better understand friendships and the dynamics of the classroom.

Health and Safety of Young School-Age Children

It is important that children have a physical examination before entering school. In fact, many school systems require it and will not allow children to attend school without a tuberculin skin test and immunizations against measles, mumps, rubella (German measles), diphtheria, tetanus, pertussis (whooping cough), polio, chicken-pox, and hepatitis B. Eye, ear, and dental examinations also are encouraged at this time. Finding any vision, hearing, or other problems before school begins will help children achieve more at school.

Getting to and from school safely

Getting to school is one of the most important events of the day for school-age children. If children will be walking, they should be taught to walk safely. Here are a few tips:

- Don't allow younger children to cross streets alone.
- Model and teach good pedestrian behaviour.
- Teach children to make eye contact with drivers—to make sure drivers see them—before crossing in front of a stopped car.
- Teach children to cross streets at corners, using traffic signals and designated crossings whenever possible.
- Teach children to look left, right, and left again when crossing a street and teach them to continue looking as they cross.
- Teach children never to run into the street.
- Ensure children are wearing reflective materials if walking at dusk and/or dawn.
- Where there are no pavements, children should walk facing traffic.

If children this age must walk alone, they should be taught to go directly to and from school without stops or side trips. They also should be told to never accept rides from strangers or even to stop to talk to strangers. These instructions should be given not in a frightening manner but matter-of-factly, so that children learn them just as they learn any other rule. Children also should know their full name and street address before they begin school, in case they get lost.

In some communities, children take a school bus. Generally, these buses pick children up at designated corners. Here are some school-bus safety tips. If children will be taking the bus, parents should go over these tips with them.

- Arrive at the bus stop early. Wait for the bus to come to a complete

Whether children walk to school or take the bus, they need to learn basic safety rules.

stop before approaching it. Watch for cars, and avoid the bus driver's blind spot.

- Stay seated on the bus at all times and keep the head and arms inside the bus while riding.
- When getting off the bus, wait until the bus comes to a complete stop. Where fitted, use the handrail to avoid falls.
- Remind children to cross the street at least 3 metres in front of a school bus. Children should wait for adults on the same side of the street as the school bus loading and unloading zone.

In addition, parents can check to see that someone on the bus is responsible for helping younger children board and exit. They should also check whether the bus is in good condition, whether the driver is reputable and qualified, and whether the roads travelled are safe. If in doubt, parents should contact a school official.

Dealing with common illnesses

Communicable diseases are quite common during the school-age years. Some can be avoided by vaccination, but parents of school-age children must learn to take in their stride the usual run of colds, sore throats, and coughs.

If children have been exposed to a communicable disease such as measles or chickenpox, a teacher or school nurse will probably send a note home informing parents of the fact and explaining what symptoms to look for. If children develop the symptoms, they should be kept home from school and seen by a doctor, if necessary.

Another common health problem in schools is head lice. Lice are tiny insects that infest the body. Head lice infestations have nothing to do with cleanliness. Lice spread from person to person easily, and anyone can get them. They adhere to hair and fibres and lay their eggs near hair shafts. The larvae that hatch, called nits, may look like dandruff. Lice produce substances that irritate the skin and scalp and can cause severe itching.

If a child at school has head lice, a note will go home to the parents of all children in the classroom, describing how to check for and treat lice. All children who have come in contact with someone who has head lice should be examined. Head lice are most commonly found on the scalp behind the ears and near the neckline at the back of the neck. The symptoms of infestation include a tickling feeling of something moving in the hair, itching caused by an allergic reaction to the bites, irritability, and sores on the head caused by scratching. If parents are unsure whether children have head lice, the child should be checked by a doctor or the school nurse.

Effective treatment for head lice can be obtained from a pharmacist.

Common Concerns

Unless children have attended a preschool or playgroup, the early school years present a new social environment and challenges unlike any they have ever had before. At home, it was taken for granted that they belonged and were accepted. This gave them a natural security. Certainly at home, they had to adapt to parents and brothers and sisters. However, the home atmosphere is unlike the challenge and interaction provided by contact with 20 to 30 classmates. Because of these new conditions, differences related to sex and age may become apparent, and certain problems may appear in children's lives.

Understanding sex differences

Girls may appear more mature than boys when they start school because they have a more rapid maturation rate than boys do during these years. Physically and emotionally, girls are likely to become organized and ready to work with symbolic and abstract tasks sooner than boys are. However, both boys and girls are ready to learn and to share knowledge.

Differences in the abilities of children in a classroom can be helpful to teachers. Consider the following situation: Patty can print her name correctly when she starts school, while Darren, who is the same age, may only recognize the first letter of his name. This does not mean that Patty is the brighter of the two. It may mean merely that someone took the time to teach her what she knows, and she may have been eager to learn this. Darren, on the other hand, may solve building problems easily when playing with blocks or use colours imaginatively. Having classmates who can print their names and a helpful teacher may encourage him to learn. He may also discover that he can use his skills and share his knowledge with other children.

Regarding age differences

No matter how bright children may be, it may make a difference whether they have lived barely five years or almost six years when they enter school. Being younger than most classmates can place some children at a disadvantage.

Suppose September 1 is the cutoff date for entering school. Children who became 5 years old on September 2 of the previous school year will be in the same class with children who turn 5 on September 1 of the current year. Children entering school at nearly six years are likely to be better co-ordinated, more able to control impulses, and more able to concentrate on a learning task.

Regardless of intellectual ability, some first-year children cannot bridge the gap between themselves and their older, more physically mature classmates. They also may have difficulty conforming to the arbitrary learning timetable of many schools. Younger children should be observed for the development of social and other school-related readiness skills. If they remain far behind their classmates in acquiring these skills, a developmental evaluation should be considered.

Coping with school problems

School is such an important part of children's lives that all children face some problems in the many years that they spend there. Therefore, parents and teachers must stay in close communication.

Problems that have their origin in school may become apparent only at home. For example, children who operate under tension all day long at school may seem earnest and conscientious to their teachers. Parents may be the only ones to see the outbursts that reflect the strain these children are feeling. Similarly, some children may appear at home to be working smoothly. Teachers, watching these children in a differ-

ent setting and in comparison with other children the same age, may be first to notice that a problem exists. All schools offer a time for parents and teachers to discuss problems. Take advantage of this.

Dealing with unwillingness to go to school

The first sign of a school problem may be an unwillingness to go to school. Some children starting school show their fear of school openly. They cry, say that they hate school, and are unwilling to leave home. Sometimes unwillingness to go to school shows in disguised form through frequent complaints of illness or prolonged dawdling and other delaying tactics. A fear or dislike of school can be a troubling problem.

The causes can be many, and they vary from child to child. The only good solution is the one that gets to the root of the difficulty. Some children may be unwilling to go to school because they have not had sufficient experience in being away from home; others because they find the large group setting over-whelming. Still others have fears about their school experience, such as riding alone on the bus, often having to deal with aggressive children on their own, or using the school toilets. The unwillingness

Some children deal with the demands of the classroom more easily than others.

also can be a sign that children are experiencing learning difficulties.

When parents and teachers begin to talk together and pool their information, they usually can uncover the difficulties and make plans that help children identify the problems, cope with them, and possibly solve them. The parents' attitudes are important while this search is going on. On the one hand, they must feel sympathetic to children who have problems. Life can be uncomfortable when something is going wrong. On the other hand, parents must have confidence that problems can be solved, and they must communicate this. When parents assure their children that they stand by them and that they will help them find solutions to their problems, they help build children's self-confidence and security. Of course, children only remain confident and secure when their parents follow through on their assurances to help.

Coping with problems related to success and failure

As children move further in their school careers, more difficulties are likely to stem from their successes and failures in academic work and from relationships with classmates and teachers. Children are like most adults. They cannot go through day after day of failure, not liking their assigned tasks, and not enjoying people with whom they associate, without feeling unhappy. Adults often change jobs when they feel this way. Most children cannot physically leave school. Their only alternative is to leave mentally—to daydream, give up, or rebel.

Again, there is no single answer to every child's trouble. A patient, mutual search by parents and teacher is the only wise procedure. A physical difficulty, with vision or hearing in particular, is sometimes a cause. Schoolwork puts the first great strain on hearing and vision. A complete physical examination is often a wise first step.

Children vary greatly in their ability to do schoolwork. They vary in intelligence, growth rate, and ability to handle specific kinds of subject matter. Possibly, without meaning to, either parents at home or teachers at school may be asking more of children than they are able to do. When expectations are too high, children almost always do not succeed as well as they could. A school's solution is sometimes to readjust its programmes, aiming more realistically at goals that children can achieve. Parents sometimes must adjust their expectations at home so that children feel successful and self-assured.

Some children have problems because they are underachievers. They have considerably more ability than they use, and they glide through their days, operating on only a small part it. On the face of it, this may not seem like a problem. However, children are much more content when they work up to their ability. Unchallenged, these children can turn to misbehaviour, such as being disruptive in class or bullying, that reflects their discontent.

It is easier to overlook children who are underachieving than those who are failing. Failing children quickly attract adult attention. Underachievers can slide by unnoticed. Parents and teachers need to talk together so that such problems are not ignored. A parent's account, for example, of a child's unusual persistence and success with a hobby or out-of-school activity may signal that the child has more ability than the school has tapped.

Coping with family problems and school

The demands of schoolwork sometimes uncover tension children are feeling at home. Children who worry about some aspect of their family life have difficulty concentrating and meeting the rigours of academic work. These difficulties may well go unnoticed before school. Once in school, however, teachers and other staff may spot the problems and look for ways to treat them. Families seeking help with problems may be able to turn to their communities for assistance. Many communities have child guidance centres that can help with family problems.

Understanding social problems

School is not for exclusively academic work. A school is a social center, too. Children's social acceptance or rejection plays a major role in their school life, and it often has repercussions on how well they learn.

Problems in children's social life are perhaps the hardest of all for adults to solve. Adults cannot force children to like one another. They can, however, sometimes help children to be more likable. Teaching children who are "picked on" some skills that other children value is one useful approach. Helping children to make friends by inviting classmates home after school is another way. Teachers also can use seating arrangements or school activities to help bring together children who may learn to like each other.

Finding solutions to school problems

As with all problems involving human interaction, children's school problems take time, patience, and wisdom to solve. In some instances, it takes a long time to work out a solution. Some of the factors that can be involved—for example, large class size, a teacher's long-established way of teaching, or a family's way of treating a child—cannot be modified overnight.

Parents and teachers must feel good will and be patient in working together if answers are to be found. It is important to recognize, too, that there are some problems children have to solve for themselves. In these instances, parents, teachers, and school administrators can only assist by helping children acquire the tools to deal with such problems.

Enjoying Young School-Age Children

Between the ages of 5 and 8, most children are open, energetic, and easy to get along with. It is a prime time for adults to help set children on a positive course in school. These early school years are formative years in children's lives and can serve as a foundation for good pre-teen and teenage behaviour. Here are some suggestions on how to make the most of children's early school years.

- Tailor expectations to fit children's abilities; then they will be encour-

aged to continue learning. If children are expected to meet unrealistic goals, they could become discouraged and disinterested in school.

- Emphasize the positive. Stress the things children can do and do not overemphasize achievement, especially in school. Children should not be told that they have to be the best. Instead, they should be told to try their best.

- Do not give children rewards for good results. Such rewards make

Assigning simple chores and praising responsible behaviour are good ways to help children take on and meet responsibilities.

children believe they must always be rewarded for doing well.

- Establish a good relationship with children's teachers. If children can do better work in school, parents should discuss the problem with teachers. Teachers can suggest effective ways to help children succeed in school.

- Continue reading to children. School-age children like stories and enjoy being read to. Reading sessions also help parents build a positive relationship with children, which can help in later years when the lines of communication between parents and children become more difficult. Listening to stories can also help improve children's comprehension and build vocabulary. Children can understand and enjoy language and ideas in books that they cannot yet read on their own.

- Good communication with children requires good listening skills. If children have something to say, parents need to take the time to listen, even if what children have to say seems of little importance.

- Help children develop a sense of responsibility. Assign some chores—drying dishes, taking the rubbish out, making the bed, keeping a clean room. Also, recognize and encourage responsible behaviour by praise. Remember that responsible behaviour also includes such everyday events as getting up and going to school and coming home promptly after school.

- Give children choices in hobbies or weekend activities. Do not force such things as taking dancing or music lessons solely because other children the same age are taking them. Respect the uniqueness and individuality of each child.

- Children need help that allows them to develop their own abilities. Too much help may make them overly dependent. Too little help may result in feelings of inadequacy or frustration. Give children the right kind of help. For example, if a child writes a letter and asks for help in spelling certain words, give help with only those words. Do not rewrite, correct, or criticize the letter.

The most important way to help school-age children be successful is to accept them as they are and inspire them to become what they want to be. And what do most children want? They want to be liked, to have interesting work to do, and to be respected. This is human and universal and highly possible if the home and school work together to achieve this end.

For Special Consideration

At one time or another, parents face special challenges related to family upheavals or to children's health and education needs. This section includes discussions of a number of challenges that parents of young children often face. It also offers ways to help parents deal with these challenges and suggests places to find further assistance.

Following the Growth of Young Children

Physical growth begins with conception. It is influenced by many factors, some of which we are only beginning to understand. The interaction between genetics and environment results in a range of possibilities for children's height.

Assessing growth

After age 2 or 3, children begin to assume their individual growth patterns, and they grow at the rate that they will follow until just before puberty. At age 3, children grow 7 to 8 centimetres per year, and between ages 4 and 9, they grow 5 to 6 centimetres per year. Growth rates of less than 5 centimetres per year after age 2 signal the need for medical assessment. Because absolute heights at any given age may vary, it is the pattern of growth that needs to be assessed.

The growth in height and weight for boys and girls at different ages is shown on the growth charts on the following pages. Typical growth is shown by the heavy centre line, and faster and slower rates by the lines above and below it. The variations in the curves show that there are periods of rapid and slow growth. After the fast growth of the first few years, the changes become more gradual and then fairly steady.

The most valuable tool for assessing children's growth is a well-kept growth chart. The most widely used charts show age marked along the bottom and height and weight marked along the sides. Children's height and weight should be measured and recorded during each medical checkup.

Looking at growth differences

The growth patterns of boys and girls are different. In the first 2 years, boys are slightly taller than girls. After that, until puberty, their heights are similar. Girls' skeletal ages—the degree to which their bones have matured—are generally more advanced than are those of boys. Children who are overweight often grow faster and reach puberty earlier than other children.

Children's rates of growth are not even. They may vary from year to year and are often fastest in the spring and summer. For this reason, growth evaluations should extend for six months to a year.

Coping with short stature

Children who are not growing at an appropriate rate should be evaluated by their doctors. Some children may be short because they come from a short family, and the genetic potential for height is small. Other children have a delay in puberty or a delayed growth spurt,

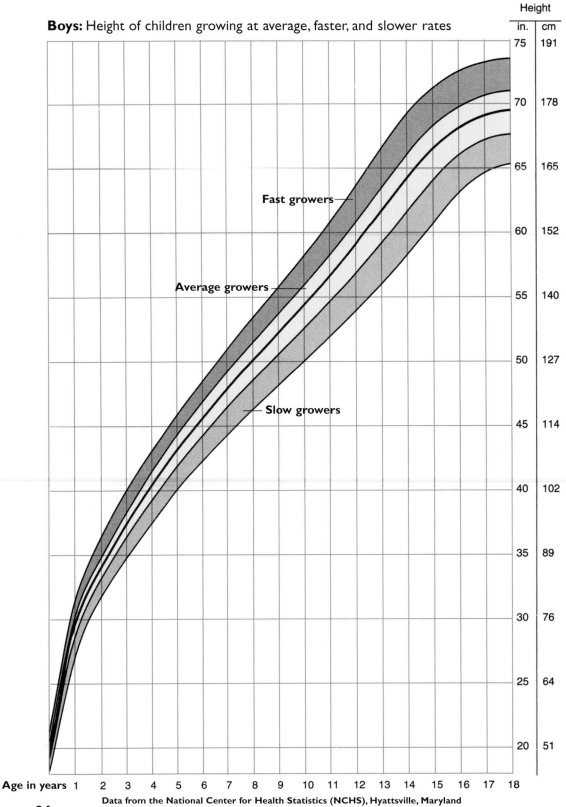

Boys: Height of children growing at average, faster, and slower rates

Height
in. | cm

75 | 191
70 | 178
65 | 165

Fast growers

60 | 152

Average growers

55 | 140
50 | 127

Slow growers

45 | 114
40 | 102
35 | 89
30 | 76
25 | 64
20 | 51

Age in years 1 2 3 4 5 6 7 8 9 10 11 12 13 14 15 16 17 18

Data from the National Center for Health Statistics (NCHS), Hyattsville, Maryland

86

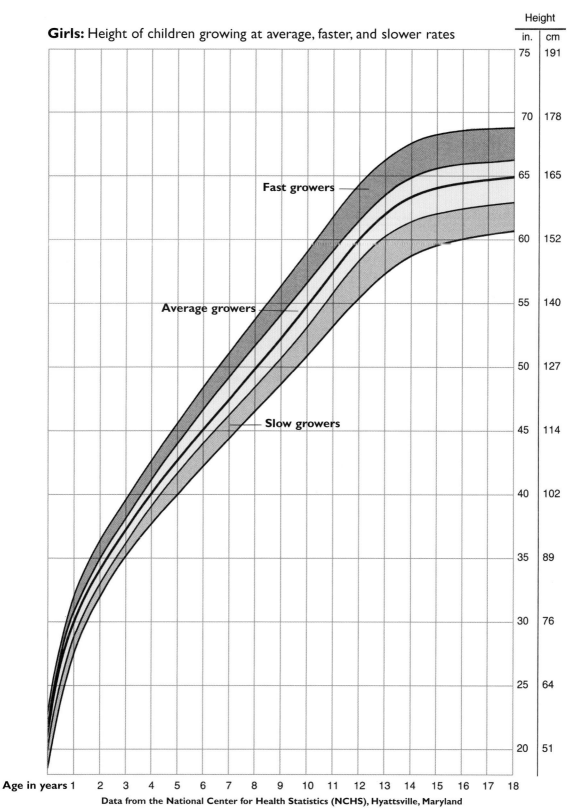

Girls: Height of children growing at average, faster, and slower rates

Height

in.	cm
75	191
70	178
65	165
60	152
55	140
50	127
45	114
40	102
35	89
30	76
25	64
20	51

Fast growers

Average growers

Slow growers

Age in years 1   2   3   4   5   6   7   8   9   10   11   12   13   14   15   16   17   18

Data from the National Center for Health Statistics (NCHS), Hyattsville, Maryland

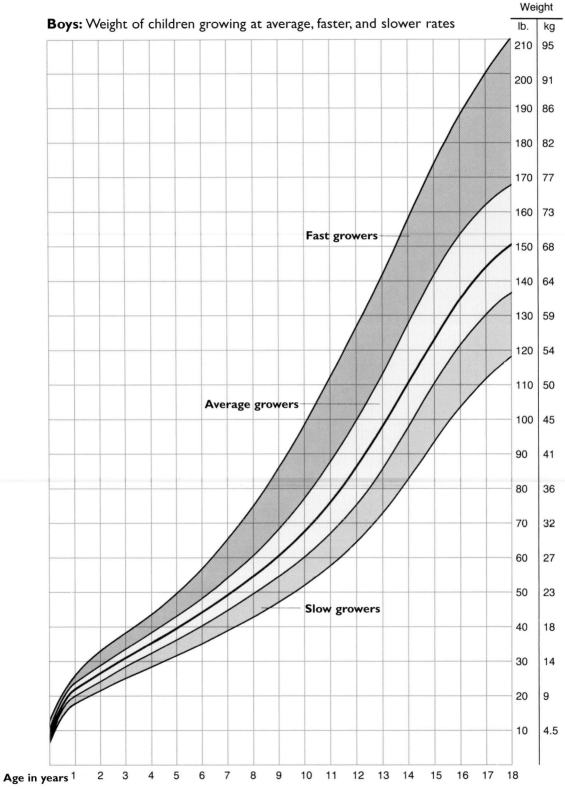

Boys: Weight of children growing at average, faster, and slower rates

Weight

| lb. | kg |

Fast growers

Average growers

Slow growers

Age in years

Data from the National Center for Health Statistics (NCHS), Hyattsville, Maryland

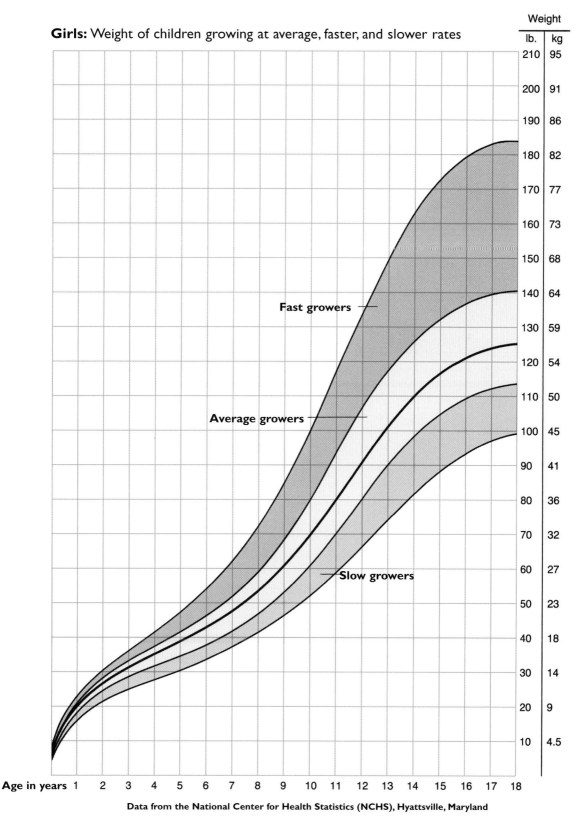

Girls: Weight of children growing at average, faster, and slower rates

Weight

lb.	kg
210	95
200	91
190	86
180	82
170	77
160	73
150	68
140	64
130	59
120	54
110	50
100	45
90	41
80	36
70	32
60	27
50	23
40	18
30	14
20	9
10	4.5

Fast growers

Average growers

Slow growers

Age in years 1 2 3 4 5 6 7 8 9 10 11 12 13 14 15 16 17 18

Data from the National Center for Health Statistics (NCHS), Hyattsville, Maryland

89

a condition called constitutional growth delay. These children are shorter than their peers but eventually reach normal height.

Worldwide, the most common cause of short stature is poor nutrition. A deprived environment can also cause it. Other causes include diseases of the heart, lungs, pancreas, kidneys, and digestive tract, and such endocrine disorders as a lack of thyroid hormone or a lack or partial deficiency of growth hormone. Too much cortisol, a stress hormone, also can cause short stature.

Children may be small for other reasons. Intrauterine growth retardation—slow growth before birth—may be caused by an infection during pregnancy or by a pregnant woman's use of alcohol, tobacco, or drugs. Chromosomal abnormalities can cause short stature. Skeletal abnormalities or bone disease also can affect the size and shape of bones. Occasionally the causes are not completely clear.

Therapy for short stature is directed at the underlying medical condition. Most growth hormone deficiencies can be treated by a paediatric endocrinologist. Children who are short because of delayed puberty, especially boys, also may benefit from medical intervention.

Coping with tall stature

Just as there are small children, there are about as many who are taller than most of their peers.

Most tall children have tall parents. Tall boys rarely complain about their size. However, tall girls may feel ill at ease. Our society seems to expect girls to be shorter than boys. Children who are growing abnormally fast should be checked by their doctors.

Abnormal height is most often caused by an endocrine disease or genetic condition. Growth hormone excess may be caused by a small tumour in the pituitary gland. A more common cause of unusually fast growth is early puberty. Genetic conditions that cause tall stature are rare, and they often include abnormal body proportions.

Dealing with emotional factors of growth

Some children with tall or short stature are emotionally troubled by their condition. Parents can boost children's self-esteem by emphasizing other characteristics, such as intelligence, personality, and talents. Children should be helped to see that their value doesn't come from height but from other qualities. Children who are very self-conscious about their size may need additional help in coping. In some cases, evaluation and treatment by a mental health professional may be necessary.

Choosing Day Care

Increasingly, parents need day care for their children while they work. Many parents are uncertain about what type of care they should seek. What day-care options are available for parents, and what are the advantages and disadvantages of each?

Types of day care for younger children

The types of day care available for younger children vary from country to country and from region to region. They may be known as nursery schools, playschools, playgroups, day nurseries, or kindergartens. In-home care, or child minding, is also available to many parents who work.

Many working parents enrol their children in a day-care centre. Different day-care centres have different sponsors, including churches, schools, colleges, independent owners, and employers. Regardless of what type of day-care centre parents choose, there are some things to consider:

- The centre should be licensed and inspected regularly for health, safety, cleanliness, staffing, and programme content. Just because a day-care centre is licensed does not mean it is regularly inspected. Parents should check to see how often the centre had announced and unannounced inspections in the past year and what was checked. To find out about regulations in their area, parents can contact the local social services department.
- Centre staff should have basic training and experience in early childhood development. Parents can check to see if centres are accredited.
- Age-appropriate toys, a daily schedule, and joyful interactions between children and staff should all be evident. Parents should be able to make unannounced visits to the centre to see their children and should be notified promptly if their children get sick or injured.

The staff of a good day-care centre has training and experience in early childhood development.

A good day-care centre that meets the above criteria is often costly because its professional staff commands good wages and its material expenses are high. And day-care centres are often open only during certain hours.

Some parents choose family day care, or child minders. In family day care, an adult cares for a small group of children in his or her own home. Usually, this adult is a mother with her own children. Some caregivers are licensed or registered and have their home visited by an inspector. However, since many day-care homes are not regulated, there is no assurance that they meet safety and health codes. Here are some things parents can look for when considering family day care:

- Is the home clean and safe?
- Are the caregiver and the caregiver's children healthy?
- Is television watching limited to one or two hours a day?
- How does the caregiver handle meals and discipline?
- How many children, including the caregiver's children, are in the home at one time? A child-care home should not have more than six children per adult caregiver. The total number of children should be even fewer when infants and toddlers are included.
- Is there backup care for emergency situations?
- What kind of training—if any—does the caregiver have? Many home-care providers will not have any formal training, but they may have years of experience doing day care or of caring for their own children.

There are some advantages to family day care over day-care centres. It is often less expensive than day-care centres. They are also likely to be located near the children's own homes, necessitating less travel time and fewer early-morning awakenings for sleepy children.

Most providers of family day-care homes are dedicated people who truly wish to give the best care. However, one advantage of day-care centres over family day care can be reliability. Most centres are open five days a week no matter what. Caregivers in family day-care settings may have to suspend their services if they or one of their children become sick or if they wish to take a holiday.

Another option for day care is to hire an in-home babysitter or nanny. In-home care can be very convenient. Many in-home caregivers can arrange their schedules to match parents' needs. Since the caregiver comes to the home, children do not have to adjust to a new setting and parents don't have to worry about travel time. Having their children at home gives parents greater control over their children's environment, as well. Also, children can receive more individual attention, especially if the caregiver is not expected to do housework. In-home care may lessen children's exposure to seasonal illnesses, because they are exposed to fewer children.

Skilled in-home caregivers can be hard to find and can be expensive. And there are other considerations. Parents need to have a backup plan for times when the caregiver is sick or goes on holiday. Parents must judge the caregiver's character, health, and skill. This makes personal references very important. In some communities, local agencies may provide training, placement, and supervision for in-home care-givers.

Which type of care is best? There is no easy answer. When choosing any kind of day care, parents should consider the following:

- **Quality of relationships.** Do the children really seem to like and enjoy the caregiver? Is the caregiver especially trained in taking care of children?

- **Location.** How far will the care be from home? From work? Is it convenient for both parents? Can both parents easily get there in an emergency?

- **Hours.** What hours of care are needed? What happens if parents are late?

- **Alternative arrangements.** What happens if children are sick? What happens if the caregiver cannot come? What if the day-care centre is closed?

- **Consistency.** Are the caregiver's policies on meals, discipline, and toilet training the same as those at home? Will children be able to have a long-term, stable relationship with the caregiver?

Choosing day care for school-age children

Some school-age children need day care before and after school. Before- and after-school facilities may be located in a day-care centre or family day-care home, or with a sitter.

Dealing with day-care problems

It is the parents' responsibility to ensure that their children receive the best care. Parents need to talk with caregivers regularly. They should plan to spend time with their children and caregivers every day, both before they leave and when they return. When problems occur, the home caregiver or staff should be able and willing to help. If problems persist, and parents suspect their child's health or safety is in question, they should find another child-care arrangement right away.

Children, Television, and the Internet

Television affects the way children spend their time and what and how they learn. Many children also spend time playing video games and using the Internet. Are these activities safe for children? What can parents do to control the influence of these activities?

Watching television

Television provides people with a wide range of new experiences. Without leaving their homes, TV viewers can see how people in far-off lands look and live. They can glimpse real-life tragedies and moments of great triumph.

While there is little agreement about how television specifically affects young people, it clearly has an impact on them. Young children, who learn by observing, will try out some of the behaviours they see on TV, both positive and negative. For this reason, children who watch programmes containing violence tend to behave more aggressively. Children also may be influenced by the sexual behaviour they see on television, adopting it at a far earlier age than their parents want.

Many social scientists believe that young people also form false impressions from watching a lot of television. They may come to believe in the stereotypes they see and form prejudices, or they may be disappointed in their own less-than-idyllic family life. Television rarely shows the effort that goes into successful lives, so children may not understand that success generally comes through hard work and sacrifice. It also does not help them understand the consequences of actions, including violent acts.

Aside from leaving people with unrealistic impressions, television viewing takes time from important leisure activities, such as reading, conversation, social gatherings, and exercise. Advertisements for products also influence children, increasing their desires for material goods.

Living with television

Parents can do a great deal to control the influence of TV on children's lives:

- Limit the amount of television children watch each day. Children need to learn that watching TV is a privilege; it is not a right.
- Forbid children to watch violent and overly sexual programmes.
- Avoid using television as an electronic babysitter. Instead, parents should look for other ways to engage their children if they are busy.
- Watch television with children and take the opportunity to teach them about what they see.

Like TV watching, Internet use needs safe limits and guidance from parents.

Parents can also avoid watching a lot of television themselves. By being good role models, they can diminish television's importance in family life. It is worth the effort!

Using the Internet

The Internet is a vast computer network that connects many of the world's businesses, institutions, and people. It has made huge amounts of information accessible to more people than ever before.

While the Internet is a great tool, there are questions about children's use of it. Not all information on the Internet is accurate, and some is deliberately misleading. Many parents are concerned about violent or pornographic material. They worry about possible criminals lurking in "chat rooms," through which people send messages to each other, and seeking to arrange face-to-face meetings with unsuspecting victims.

Living with the Internet

Just as parents have rules about watching TV, it is important to have rules about using the Internet. To keep children's time on the Internet safe, productive, and fun, parents should follow these guidelines:

- Set limits on the amount of time children can spend online each day or each week.
- Do not let "surfing" the Internet take the place of homework, outdoor play, or friends.
- Make sure children know that people online are not always who they say they are and that online information is not necessarily private.
- Teach children to never give out personal information, never use a credit card online without permission, never share passwords, never arrange a face-to-face meeting, never respond to messages that make them feel confused or uncomfortable, and never use bad language or send nasty messages online.
- Make a point of participating in children's online time. Stay involved and monitor what children are doing online.

Special programmes known as parental control software can help parents block access to sites that may be unsuitable for children. Education associations, Internet providers, and libraries often have information on blocking software.

Moving

Moving can be an exciting adventure or a disruption in children's lives. However, since children usually follow the lead of their parents, the degree of excitement or uneasiness that children feel will depend largely on their parents' attitudes and explanations.

Most children, especially those who have close friends or who have formed strong ties to people, places, and the routines of their neighbourhood, will feel sad at leaving. But beyond such normal regrets, how parents act can make children eager to tackle a new and interesting life experience.

Preparing children for a move

If children are old enough to understand, parents should talk about the move often and give as much information as possible beforehand. More lead time means more time for children to get used to the idea. Parents should answer questions completely and honestly and be receptive to children's reactions, positive or negative. It might be helpful for parents to share their own thoughts about the move, or to talk about how they handled similar experiences as young children.

If possible, parents should give children a clear picture of what it may be like to live in the new place.

If the family is planning to move to another part of the country, or to another country, parents and children can study maps and read stories and articles about the area. This will give children a better idea of where they will be living.

Parents also should discuss any aspects of the move that may present problems for children, such as a different climate or the lack of certain things they are accustomed to in their present home. Whenever possible, parents need to explain unfamiliar local customs, so that children will take an interest in the different ways people do things. These explanations will help children learn to respect differences.

Children's reactions to moving are likely to mirror their parents' feelings.

Involving children in planning and decision-making—to an appropriate extent—can help them feel that they are participating in the move rather than having it forced upon them.

Coping with problems

Even with the best preparation, some children may have deep emotional reactions to moving. Often, anxiety over the welfare of a pet that cannot be taken along may precipitate an emotional crisis. Parents can relieve anxiety by allowing children to help find a good home for the pet.

Leaving friends may be especially hard on children. Joining small community or religious groups that usually welcome newcomers may help children feel more at ease. Many people have had some experience with moving to a new community, and they expect to welcome newcomers. The friendly atmosphere makes it easier for children to meet new friends and develop new interests.

If children are shy or timid or show much uneasiness, they will need a lot of support when they enter a new school. Parents should take children to school before classes begin and introduce them to the teachers and, if possible, some future classmates. If children have problems with schoolwork or physical problems such as poor coordination, vision, or hearing, the school should know about them. The school should also know about children's abilities. Most teachers want to be helpful, but to do their best, they must be aware of special needs.

Sometimes children appear to have adjusted to a move without difficulty, but they have an emotional slump after the initial excitement has worn off. Perhaps the new school is not as challenging or as stimulating as the old school, and children are bored. Or perhaps it is quite a bit more challenging than the previous one, and children have trouble keeping up. Or they could find it hard to make new friends. Parents can help by talking to teachers. Together, they might be able to help children adjust by helping them find more interests or more congenial friends.

It is not unusual for well-adjusted children to feel lonely, restless, and moody after a move. But if children were already unhappy, the move may increase their anxiety. Parents may have to turn to someone trained to help them understand the basic causes of their children's unhappiness.

Most children, however, settle into the new community within a period of months. Their adjustment is helped considerably if the experience of the move has given them the secure feeling that wherever they live, their family can make a home under all kinds of circumstances. This is a fine way to establish the emotional security that will support them throughout life.

Travelling with Young Children

A family holiday is a special time, but it may take some creativity to make getting there fun for children. Parents can plan some activities to help keep children contented on a long trip.

- If the trip is long, start at a time when children will be likely to sleep for all or part of the trip.
- Pack activities to pass the time. Paper and crayons or felt-tipped pens for drawing are favourites with most children. A tray with legs will make them easier for children to use. A tray also comes in handy for doing jigsaw puzzles and for building with blocks.
- Bring a small cassette recorder along with some favourite music and story tapes. Children also love blank tapes for recording songs they sing or stories they make up along the way.
- Play games. Many popular children's games come in travel-sized

Belting up is a good start to any holiday trip.

editions, and card games are easy to take along.

- Prepare a list of things children can look for along the ride, and see how many they can find.
- Take along small surprises for children to open and play with as a reward for behaving well.
- When travelling by car, plan to stop every few hours to allow children to run off pent-up energy. Knowing that there will be frequent breaks will help children remain safely seated. One of the most difficult parts of travelling with children is having to confine them to their car seats or seat belts, but remember that "belting up" is the only safe way to travel on both short and long trips.
- Pack favourite snack foods such as dry cereal, crisps, raisins, and juice. If the weather is nice, pack a picnic lunch and plan to stop at an outdoor rest area, where children can run around and burn off some energy.
- Bring moist wipes for a quick, sanitary clean-up; a change of clothes in case the travelling clothes become particularly messy; and a favourite stuffed animal or blanket for comfort.
- Always have a first-aid kit while travelling. Childhood accidents occur when travelling because of changes in routine and environ-

ment. Items to bring along include bandages, an antibiotic spray, and important health information, such as a list of allergies, other medical conditions, or regular medication.

- If travelling by plane, plan to take a nonstop flight and request seats in the first row or on the aisle, where there is more room. Although airlines usually provide earlier boarding for those flying with children, this may not be the best option with active infants or toddlers because they will be confined longer. It may be better to board later and let children run off energy. During take-off and landing, encourage children to drink liquids or chew gum (if age-appropriate) to equalize pressure and prevent ear discomfort. If children are prone to ear infections, get their ears checked before flying.

Children are usually thrilled about travelling and going on a holiday, but parents need to keep in mind that changes in children's routines, coupled with added excitement, may alter their sleeping patterns and also cause changes in their behaviour. However, these are temporary disruptions and should not interfere with the fun of a family holiday. Life will go back to normal after returning home.

Protecting Children from Poisons

Children explore their environment by touching, smelling, and tasting. They often don't pause to consider whether or not something is good for them. They just try it. So it is not surprising that every year, hospitals treat thousands of children who have ingested harmful substances.

Cosmetics are the leading poisonous substance swallowed by small children. Other leading substances, in order, are plants, soaps and detergents, cold medications, analgesics, and vitamins. Child-resistant packaging on some household items has helped prevent some poisonings. Unfortunately, no packaging is absolutely childproof.

Observing some safety rules, and checking or cleaning out areas of the house, can help protect children from poisoning. Here are some rules to follow and tips for ways to make the home safer:

- Keep all medicines and chemicals out of the reach of children. Discard any potential poisons that are of little use. Children are more sensitive than adults to poison, and a smaller amount may cause death. Store all aftershaves, colognes, and perfumes—which have a high alcohol content—and all super glues out of reach.
- Don't refer to medication as sweets.
- Buy medications and household products with child-resistant caps.
- Never leave alcoholic drinks within children's reach.
- Always read the warning labels on hazardous products.
- Keep all products in their original containers and avoid purchasing toxic substances, such as household cleaners, that have appealing fragrances like lemon or almond.
- Never put inedible or hazardous products in cups or other containers that would normally be used for food or drinks.
- Avoid taking medication in the presence of children.
- Teach young children not to eat or drink anything unless it is given to them by an adult they know.
- Do not depend on close adult supervision to keep children safe. Children move quickly and can get into things before an adult can intervene.
- Be alert for repeat occurrences. For some reason, children exposed to dangerous substances or poisoning are likely to try a second ingestion within one year.
- Keep toxic plants out of reach.
- Maintain heating appliances in good working order. This will help prevent both natural gas and carbon monoxide poisoning.

Parents should teach children to recognize poisonous substances. Danger symbols on containers can help.

- Keep the telephone numbers of a doctor and hospitals with accident and emergency departments near your telephone.
- If children swallow a non-food item or are exposed to toxic fumes, call a doctor or hospital. Make sure to have the container handy in case there are questions about the substance.
- Do not attempt self-directed home treatment of poisoned children. In some cases, inducing vomiting can worsen the condition. Do not rely on a poison treatment chart. Call a doctor or hospital.
- Keep a one-ounce bottle of syrup of ipecac in the home medicine chest. This is used to induce vomiting in some poisoning situations. However, do not use syrup of ipecac without professional advice.
- If you are unsure what caused the poisoning, save any vomit or urine children produce. It may be needed for analysis in a hospital accident and emergency department.

One situation for which adults should begin treatment before seeking professional help is eye contamination. An eye exposed to an irritant should be flushed with lukewarm water for 15 minutes. The quickest method is to use a gentle stream of lukewarm water from a kitchen or bathroom tap. Another method is to use a jug and slowly pour water over the eye. If children fight the treatment, wrap them in a blanket or sheet to keep them from struggling.

Another area in which treatment can be given before calling for professional assistance is skin exposed to acids, alkalis, petroleum products, or insecticides. Remove the children's clothes and bathe the affected area thoroughly. Discard any leather or other porous materials that could have absorbed the substance.

Remember, almost all non-food substances are a potential danger to children. Keeping dangerous substances out of sight and out of reach goes a long way in protecting children against accidental poisoning.

Explaining Death to Children

Almost all children at some point ask, "What does it mean to be dead?" or "Will I die, too?" Children may want to know why and how a pet dies. They may have seen a funeral procession or heard about the death of a well-known person. Or a family member may have died.

Many parents who are willing and able to discuss almost any subject with their children become evasive and ill at ease when questioned about death. Perhaps it is because most of us would rather not think about death. But when a loved one dies, it is important that parents be prepared to talk about it.

Children usually have strong emotions about death. They may have feelings of sorrow, fear, resentment, and even guilt. They may become confused and bewildered. How parents explain death, and how they answer children's questions about death, are important. Parents should be aware that children's concepts of death change as they get older.

Between 3 and 5, children tend to think of death as a journey from which a person will soon return. Or, they may think death is a kind of going to sleep and then waking up. When told of a death, they may express sorrow but seem to forget about it soon afterwards. Parents who are unaware of this common reaction may worry that children are self-centred and heartless.

Between the ages of 5 and 9, most children accept the idea that death is irreversible, but they believe that death happens only to certain people. Around the ages of 9 or 10, children begin to understand that death happens to all living things, and they will die eventually, too.

Answering questions

No matter how difficult it may be, an open, calm answer about death is the best one. Children are not nearly as afraid of what they can understand as they are of things that are cloaked in mystery.

In explaining death, parents usually have to deal with such facts as illness, accidents, or old age. The amount of information should relate to a child's capacity to understand. For instance, if a 3-year-old wants to know why a grandparent has died, it is usually enough to say, "She was very old and very tired." A 6-year-old might be told that the grandmother was very old and tired, and that eventually everyone grows old and tired and can no longer go on living.

Some parents give evasive answers in the belief that they are guarding against pain that the truth would cause. But an evasive answer may cause problems. For example,

When a loved one dies, children need to be able to talk about their feelings.

when a grandfather dies and a 6-year-old is told that he went to sleep, the child may become fearful of going to sleep and not waking up.

Even a religious explanation is not always helpful. Few children find comfort in such explanations as "God took him". They could have feelings of resentment against God.

Children often feel that in some way or other they are responsible for the death. Parents can help children overcome such guilt.

Children are more deeply affected by some deaths than by others. When a playmate or a playmate's parent dies, children are likely to think that they might also die young or lose a parent. Parents can reassure children by stressing that few people die young. Parents also might add that friends and family will take care of their children should anything happen to them.

The death of a parent is especially difficult. Children suffer not only grief, but a loss of security. If surviving parents are in no condition to comfort children, they may feel rejected. At such times, adult relatives or friends of the family can be a source of strength and reassurance about the future. At no time should a child be told that he or she must take on adult responsibilities to make up for the absent parent.

Mourning

There are differences of opinion about children's participation in family gatherings of mourning and funeral ceremonies. A common practice in many families is to send the children to stay with friends so that they will be spared the effects of grief. In some instances, this may be wise, but often it makes children feel alone and shut out. To be with the family, yet to be protected from extreme demonstrations of grief, is often more reassuring for children than being spared the experience.

Parents faced with helping children understand a death in the family or the death of a close friend should be honest. They need to help children see that life holds some sorrow as well as joy for everyone. Children need love, affection, and understanding to get through the experience in a positive way. The value of the feeling of belonging, in sorrow as well as in joy, cannot be overemphasized.

Dealing with Behaviour Problems

At times, all children behave in ways that puzzle or worry parents. Many children may even show what seem to be symptoms of a behaviour problem. Symptoms such as aggressiveness, fears, and compulsions indicate a behaviour problem only when they are severe or occur frequently. Such severe problems are typically the result of some sort of emotional disturbance. However, before parents conclude that this is the case, they should make sure that their children do not have a physical or mental illness. Many symptoms of behaviour problems can be created or made worse by a physical or mental illness.

Understanding emotional problems

Children live in four different worlds—the world of family and home; the world of school; the world of friendships; and their inner world. Behaviour problems can occur as a result of emotional problems in all or any of these four worlds.

In the home, there normally is a bond of affection between parents, and between children and each parent. As a part of the family, children are expected to pay a reasonable amount of attention to family rules and to perform tasks that are appropriate for their age and ability.

Emotional problems may develop if there is not a good relationship with parents, if independence proceeds too slowly or too rapidly, or if family rules and tasks are ignored. Although quarrelling and jealousy between siblings are hard to take, most child development specialists typically view them as a normal part of sibling relationships.

Children spend a great deal of time in the world of school—about 1,000 hours a year. There, they are expected to perform to the best of their ability, conform socially, and develop interests in studies and other activities. Emotional problems can occur if children's performance in school does not match the expectations of parents, and in turn, the parents pressure their children to improve. The emotional problems may result in a disinterest in school. Children may start to dislike school, act out in the classroom, or fail to achieve their potential.

Childhood friendships have a tremendous impact on children's development. From such associations, children learn social customs and patterns of behaviour. Much of the ability to succeed in adult relationships grows out of the behaviour patterns that are developed during childhood. Because of the importance of healthy childhood friendships, parents should be con-

Some squabbling between brothers and sisters is normal, even in close and affectionate families.

cerned about children who are always alone or who are consistently aggressive towards other children. Such behaviours could signal an emotional problem.

The inner world of children is in some ways the most important and the most difficult to understand. This is their world of thoughts, fears, hopes, attitudes, and ambitions. When children have a strong, constant sense of not measuring up to other children, it is reasonable to assume that there may be an emotional problem.

Everyone has to face problems of one kind or another throughout life. In spite of this, well-adjusted people continue to find life a source of satisfaction. Such people are usually optimistic about the future. If this feeling of optimism never occurs in children, then emotional problems result.

Two of the most common behaviour problems in children are unrealistic fears and aggressive behaviour.

All children are afraid from time to time. Fear is a normal emotion. However, fears are unrealistic if they occur regularly in the absence of real danger. In some cases, such fears may be directly related to a frightening past experience. In other cases, they may be only indirectly related to a past event. For example, a child who feels extreme guilt may expect severe punishment and then develop an abnormal fear of death, accidents, or illness. Some fears become so

105

intense that they prevent children from carrying out normal activities.

Psychologists define aggression as angry, hostile behaviour that is intended to hurt or upset others. Such behaviour in young children can result from frustration. Children may feel frustrated if their demands are not met or if their feelings of worthiness are threatened. If the anger is intense, it may erupt into a tantrum—a common form of aggression in young children.

Other special problems of childhood also may be symptoms of emotional or physical disorders. They include hyperactivity (extreme restlessness), extreme shyness, and bed-wetting.

Finding the root of problems

If children frequently show symptoms of a behaviour disorder, parents should not ignore the symptoms and hope they will disappear in time. Children are too important for parents to rely on chance.

If their children are having behaviour problems, parents need to discuss it together. It is extremely important that the discussion take place when they are feeling good rather than when they are upset and angry because their children have behaved poorly. During the discussion, they must take a look at how their family as a group and how each individual member behaves in relation to their child with the behaviour problem.

Also, parents must be able to admit that while the ways they do things may work well with some children, and may even be necessary, they have not been successful with the emotionally disturbed child. This admission calls for a willingness to accept the fact that their parental behaviour is related to the child's difficulty, and that a change in their approach may be a solution to the problem.

There are certain types of parental behaviour that can lead to behaviour problems in children. A few are listed below. Some problems, however, have no obvious cause. Some simply stem from children's personalities. Some children become more frustrated than others and act out in different ways. Some problems are caused by a chemical imbalance that medical treatment may be able to help. Because there are many causes, consulting a health care professional is always a good idea.

Demanding perfection. Parents who demand a great deal of themselves may place unreasonable demands on their children. No matter how hard children try, their perfectionist parents are never quite satisfied or pleased. Emotional problems can often be related to this abnormal demand for perfection. Perfectionist parents should try to be less rigid about rules and look for behaviours that can be praised.

Being inconsistent. Inconsistent parents create an uncertain environment by changing rules so often that children cannot know what is expected. Most parents are inconsistent at times, but when they constantly change rules relating to children's behaviour, it is damaging to the children. Children thrive on consistency. Inconsistent parents should decide important basic household rules, write them down, and try to stick to them.

Overprotecting children. Overprotective parents shield children excessively, either because they cannot bear their children growing up or because of their own concern for dangers in the world. This attitude may inhibit the development of independent skills. Parents who recognize that overprotection is a problem should talk to other parents and child development experts about ways to allow children more independence.

Being indulgent. Never setting limits may also be a source of a behaviour disorder. Children are much more comfortable when they have rules to follow. Rules prepare them to face the many situations in which individual desires must be put aside in favour of group needs.

Quarrelling. Parents also may contribute to children's problems if there is constant quarrelling.

The obvious solution is to avoid quarrelling in the presence of children.

Being uninvolved. Parents who have little to do with their children will be unable to convince their children of their love, interest, and concern. Children need models after which they can pattern their own behaviour. To be effective models, parents must be available and interested in their children. Adults who rely heavily on punishment may tend to deal with recurring problems by thinking up new and unusual punishments. If children show symptoms of a behaviour problem and have been punished a great deal, it is reasonable to assume that more punishment will only aggravate the condition. If punishment is necessary, parents should make sure that the punishment is not excessive. In addition, parents should also be sure to offer a lot of praise to reinforce good behaviour.

Working with children with behaviour problems. If parents recognize that previous methods of handling their children have been unsuccessful or even harmful, they should plan a new programme. If the children are old enough to reason with, the process will be made easier by a frank discussion when all are feeling friendly. Parents should tell their children how concerned they are and how much they want to help. They should indicate how they plan to change their behaviour, and they should agree to meet on a regular basis to discuss progress. The children should be allowed to speak freely during the discussions, and nothing they say should be held against them.

If the children's behaviour has become a problem at school, it is important that parents discuss the problem with teachers and other staff. These people are interested in the children and can offer advice and guidance. This may be extremely valuable in helping parents understand why their children are having difficulty.

Seeking professional help

It is usually difficult for parents to admit that their children may need psychological support. It is reasonable for parents to assume that they can work out some of their children's problems without outside help. If there is improvement, they should continue. However, if in a reasonable time there is no improvement, it is time to seek professional help.

If children are overly fearful or aggressive, or show such symptoms as continued hyperactivity, extreme shyness, or bed-wetting, parents should consult their child guidance clinic or family doctor. If necessary, they will be referred to a psychiatrist, a clinical psychologist, or a mental health clinic. Often an outsider with specialized training can approach the problem with greater objectivity.

When parents seek help for their children, they must be prepared to accept the fact that they may be partly responsible for the emotional problem. Parents should be willing to learn how they have contributed to the problem and work with the doctor or child guidance professional, to produce good results.

The treatment of children with behaviour problems often requires a great deal of time and patience on the part of parents and child guidance specialists. A severe behavioural problem usually takes a long time to develop, and as long a time may be required to correct it. Fortunately, most children respond favourably to treatment, especially when all members of the family are trying to help.

Learning Disabilities

Children are born with unique developmental profiles and can exhibit strengths and weaknesses in different aspects of development, such as fine and gross motor activity, attention span, memory function, language, perception, and productivity. Weaknesses in any of these areas may affect the ability of children to function well in a regular classroom environment. Such mild impairments in child development are often identified as learning disabilities. They are often first noted when children enter school and have trouble meeting the academic and social challenges of their new environment.

Learning disabilities may be expressed in a variety of symptoms, and at times it is difficult to distinguish between normal variations in children's learning styles and true learning disabilities.

Certain risk factors may predispose children to learning difficulties. Some children may have a genetic abnormality. Others may have experienced serious medical problems that damaged the central nervous system and, therefore, affected their development.

To overcome the fear of "looking bad" in the classroom, children with learning disabilities need steady support and encouragement from parents and teachers.

Exposure to toxins and infections can sometimes adversely affect the development of children's central nervous system before birth. With the vast majority of children, however, the cause of the learning disability is not easily identified.

Developmental skills

In order to function well in school, children must acquire a variety of developmental skills, including auditory and visual memory, expressive and receptive language, motor skills, attention, higher-order reasoning, and motivation. The presence or absence of these skills in the developmental profile of children can affect their performance in such academic areas as reading, spelling, science, mathematics, as well as social development.

The desire to be accepted by other children in the classroom is an important goal for most school-age children. When children enter school, they leave the security of the home for an environment where they face peer pressure every day. For most children, this change produces positive results. By interacting with other children in this new environment, they learn more about themselves, as well as about patterns of socially acceptable behaviour. But for children with learning disabilities, the change can be painful. Their main goal in the classroom is not to be embarrassed by their performance. "Looking bad" can cause children with learning disabilities to lose confidence in their abilities and lose self-esteem.

Children who constantly experience failure in the classroom express their frustration and unhappiness in different ways. Some children become socially withdrawn and depressed. Others may be disruptive in class. Children also may experience such symptoms as headaches, stomach aches, limb pains, nail biting, and wetting or soiling their clothes.

Dealing with learning disabilities

The parents' observations of their children's development in the years before school begins are often important in identifying children who may be at risk for school failure. Children who are delayed in reaching developmental milestones, especially in language skills, are more likely to have problems in school. Parents who feel that their children have marked developmental delays in language skills, attention, and such basic self-help skills as dressing, should contact their doctor. Early identification and intervention can help such children develop their full capabilities.

In most cases, however, the problems of children with learning disabilities do not become obvious until the children are in school. Teachers' concerns about children's difficulties in paying attention or learning a specific skill, such as recognizing letters, may be the parents' first clue that learning disabilities exist. If children are unable to master skills that are readily learned by classmates, a complete evaluation by an educational psychologist should be performed. This evaluation should include tests to identify the developmental skills needed to function efficiently in a classroom setting. Children should also have a physical examination, including vision and hearing screening, in order to rule out any medical causes of learning impairments. A social evaluation also should be included, since environmental factors also may affect performance.

When the evaluation is completed, parents and teachers can be provided with a description of children's developmental strengths and weaknesses, and recommendations can be made for an appropriate classroom environment and for changes in the home that would benefit children as well.

Medications are sometimes prescribed as part of the treatment of children with an attention deficit disorder (ADD), or attention deficit/hyperactivity disorder (ADHD). It is important for parents and teachers to understand that medications will not cure a learning disability, even though they sometimes help children who have serious problems with inattention and impulsive behaviour. Counselling for children and family is also sometimes recommended in order to help children deal with problems as they are encountered. With these kinds of support, and with continued observation and help, children with learning disabilities can be expected to develop academically and socially to their full capabilities.

Mental Retardation

The term "mental retardation" refers to a condition in which people have substantial limitations in their intellectual abilities. Children are diagnosed as mentally retarded if they perform far below average, both intellectually and behaviourally. They do not think, reason, remember, and learn as well as other children the same age. However, except in cases of extreme retardation, parents and teachers can help children with mental retardation develop strategies so that they need not be totally dependent on others to survive. The way the family and others treat children with mental retardation has a lot to do with whether or not they can remain emotionally healthy and well adjusted.

Mental retardation can result from any factor that hinders healthy brain development. Babies may be mentally retarded as a result of genetic errors that may or may not have been inherited or as a result of an accident that results in brain injury. Consumption of alcohol during pregnancy can lead to a condition in babies called fetal alcohol syndrome, which can cause mental retardation. Use of prescription, nonprescription, or illegal drugs also can harm developing babies' brains. Exposure before birth to certain infections, including rubella (also called German measles) and HIV, also can cause retardation. During childhood, retardation can result from such causes as brain infections, head injuries, prolonged high fevers, or lead poisoning.

To be considered mentally retarded, people must show signs of the condition before they reach 18 years of age. The most common symptom of retardation is a delay in achieving milestones of development. Many children with severe mental retardation fail to sit up or walk at the usual age for these accomplish-

A climate of family love and support is important for all children.

ments. Children with less severe retardation may be slow in learning to talk. Mild retardation may escape detection until a child starts school and has trouble learning.

Coping with mental retardation

Whenever parents are puzzled by their children's development, they should seek professional help. The family doctor can refer parents to a special clinic for a detailed diagnosis and evaluation of children's conditions. As a rule, a good diagnosis will include a thorough study of physical, psychological, and social factors involved in behaviour. When a thorough study has been made, parents feel less compelled to go from one doctor to another in the hope of finding an easy cure for the condition.

Children with mental retardation, like any children, should get good medical care and attention. They need nourishing food, plenty of sleep, immunizations, correction of any physical defects that can be corrected, and careful nursing during illness. A periodic reassessment of their condition is important.

Few parents adjust easily to the idea that their children are mentally retarded. Many parents find that talking to others in the same situation can be a great comfort. Through certain agencies and associations, parents meet to exchange ideas, discuss problems,

set up schools, and promote understanding of mental retardation.

Living with retarded children

Children with mental retardation, like all children, need to begin life with parental love in family surroundings. Today there is greater understanding of retardation and more help available in the community. Most experts recommend keeping children with mental retardation at home rather than in an institution. If parents can help them do more and more alone, they will begin to take pride and joy in their children's accomplishments, no matter how small.

The lives of children with mental retardation should be kept simple and orderly. They need to know what is expected every day. Patient teaching is required to help them learn what average children of their age learn quickly. Parents may have to repeat the same instructions, activities, and simple lessons many times before a simple idea is grasped. But children with mental retardation should not be pushed beyond their abilities. If overloaded, they may become confused, and any efforts to learn will be blocked.

Parents need patience to discipline children with mental retardation. These children need to learn rules, but what is expected should be based on their ability and development. Sometimes, parents demand better behaviour from children with mental retardation than from the other children in the family. They expect far more in the way of control and co-operation than the children can possibly offer. As with any other aspect of learning, the demand for more than the children are capable of giving will hinder rather than help.

Understanding the impact on the family

While it is not always the case, the severity of children's retardation may determine the effect their disability has on the rest of their family. If the retardation is severe, it may be necessary to leave children with mental retardation in the care of sitters on occasion so that the rest of the family can get out. The other children may become resentful if their activities are curtailed by the needs of their sibling with mental retardation.

It is a good idea for parents to train special caretakers and to keep the same ones, if possible. Students who are enrolled in special education courses at nearby colleges are often attuned to young children's needs and eager to gain first-hand experience in caring for children with mental retardation. Many areas have daycare centres and residential centres for those most retarded.

Usually, brothers and sisters reflect the attitudes and behaviour of parents toward children with mental retardation. Children with mental retardation can become scapegoats for many family problems, including problems that would exist even if the children with mental retardation were not around. Under such circumstances, a child with mental retardation will very likely not develop his or her full potential, intellectually or socially, and will have difficulty learning the skills needed to achieve some measure of independence.

On the other hand, children with mental retardation can become valued members of families, around whose needs other family members can rally and become united more strongly than ever. A child with mental retardation who is respected by parents, brothers and sisters, and relatives can return affection and develop rewarding relationships with family and friends. In such a climate of family support, the child will be able to develop social skills more fully and feel more positive about his or her very real and very important achievements.

Physical Disabilities

Physical disabilities are physical problems that will ultimately interfere with people's expectations, job performance, or relationships with their family, friends, and society in general. Some physically disabled children with normal intelligence have a good chance for a useful and satisfying life. The role of parents in helping ensure their children with physical disabilities have a satisfying life is to love and accept them. They must also help them develop self-confidence by concentrating on what they can do rather than on what they cannot do.

Caring for the disabled child at home

Physically disabled children have needs that go beyond special medical attention to their physical problems. Disabled children, like normal children, need good nutrition and immunization against disease. These children need periodic visits to the family doctor or hospital. Babies with disabilities need the same amount of cuddling and attention as normal babies. Toddlers need to explore, and preschool children should be stimulated with new experiences.

Children with disabilities, like normal children, must be given responsibilities and tasks appropriate to their age and abilities. This gives them the feeling of being trusted and needed. They also need discipline—neither more nor less than that needed by all children—to learn the limits of socially acceptable behaviour. Children with disabilities feel more secure knowing that they are expected to be as well behaved as all other children are.

Parents should refrain from rushing to help their disabled children do things that the children can do alone. But there is no harm in making things easier for them. For instance, parents can alter clothes so that children can dress and undress with as little difficulty as possible. They can arrange furniture so that the children can get around the house more easily.

Educating children with disabilities

Medical treatment and special education during early childhood help many children with physical disabilities lessen or even overcome their disabilities. For example, special education can give the child with cerebral palsy a chance to improve co-ordination and speech. A school environment also provides the opportunity for children with physical disabilities to relate to people outside the family and to learn to handle other reactions to their physical differences.

Many physically disabled children attend normal classes and school activities.

Some children with physical disabilities can attend normal school classes. Some schools have classrooms adapted to their special needs and trained teachers to instruct them. Some communities provide bus services for children who need wheelchairs, braces, or other equipment to get around.

When children are too severely disabled to attend school, schools may send teachers to their homes, or they may provide electronic or other teaching equipment. Residential schools may provide medical and educational services in cases where parents are unable to cope with disabled children at home, or where local facilities are either inadequate or nonexistent. Such schools are very much like boarding schools in that the children may return home for the holidays.

Finding help

The cost of providing treatment and special education for children with physical disabilities can become a financial burden. Many areas have government agencies that can help. Some offer financial assistance or help in planning education.

There are many agencies and groups that deal with children with disabilities. They often offer parent-education programmes to help parents face problems, understand their own attitudes, and understand the causes and the nature of their children's disabilities. Perhaps more important, parents learn they are not alone when they share their experiences with other parents of children with disabilities.

Parent-education programmes are led by qualified people in the fields of medicine and special education. Discussions, lectures, visual aids, and trips to schools and institutions for people with disabilities give parents information on the health care, discipline, and physical and psychological adjustments that are necessary in caring for children with a disability. Where such groups do not exist, some agencies have mobile units to provide parents with counselling. In time, parents become aware that their disabled children are in most ways like all other children.

Resources for Parents

There are many agencies that provide information and counselling to anyone seeking help with special problems relating to family and child health and education. Some of these agencies and organizations are privately sponsored. Others are sponsored by governments. Many of them offer pamphlets and other literature on a wide variety of topics.

Telephone directories usually list local agencies and organizations. You also can find information about local and national organizations that offer information and assistance on the Internet.

If you have difficulty finding an agency or an organization that seems equipped to meet your special needs, your doctor, the nearest hospital, the local health authority, or your spiritual adviser may be able to suggest others. A great many people have had a great deal to say about child development and related subjects dealing with child guidance, family living and the changing family, education, sex education, special needs, and health.

On November 20, 1989, the United Nations General Assembly addressed these concerns and the needs of children when it adopted the Convention on the Rights of the Child. On the next two pages is a plain language version of the official text, prepared by The Save The Children Fund and UNICEF, the United Nations Children's Fund.

The Convention on the Rights of the Child

Article 1: The Convention defines a child as a person under 18 unless national law recognizes that the age of majority is reached earlier.

Article 2: All the rights laid down in the Convention are to be enjoyed by children regardless of race, colour, sex, language, religion, political, or other opinion, national, ethnic, or social origin, property, disability, birth, or other status.

Article 3: All sections concerning the child should be in her/his best interests.

Article 4: The State's obligation to translate the rights of the Convention into reality.

Article 5: The State should respect the rights and responsibilities of parents to provide guidance appropriate to the child's capacities.

Article 6: The right to life.

Article 7: The right to a name and a nationality and, as far as possible, the right to know and to be cared for by her/his parents.

Article 8: The right to protection of her/his identity by the State.

Article 9: The right to live with her/his parents unless incompatible with her/his best interests. The right, if desired, to maintain personal relations and direct contact with both parents if separated from one or both.

Article 10: The right to leave and enter her/his own country, and other countries, for purposes of reunion with parents and maintaining the child-parent relationship.

Article 11: The right to protection by the State if unlawfully taken or kept abroad by a parent.

Article 12: The right to freely express an opinion in all matters affecting her/him and to have that opinion taken into account.

Article 13: The right to express views, and obtain and transmit ideas and information regardless of frontiers.

Article 14: The right to freedom of thought, conscience, and religion, subject to appropriate parental guidance.

Article 15: The right to meet together with other children and join and form associations.

Article 16: The right to protection from arbitrary and unlawful interference with privacy, family, home, and correspondence, and from libel and slander.

Article 17: The right of access to information and materials from a diversity of sources and of protection from harmful materials.

Article 18: The right to benefit from child-rearing assistance and child-care services and facilities provided to parents/guardians by the State.

Article 19: The right to protection from maltreatment by parents or others responsible for her/his care.

Article 20: The right to special protection if s/he is temporarily or permanently deprived of her/his family environment, due regard being paid to her/his cultural background.

Article 21: The right, in countries where adoption is allowed, to have it ensured that an adoption is carried out in her/his best interests.

Article 22: The right, if a refugee, to special protection.

Article 23: The right, if disabled, to special care, education, and training to help her/him enjoy a full life in conditions that ensure dignity and promote self-reliance and a full and active life in society.

Article 24: The right to the highest standard of health and medical care attainable.

Article 25: The right, if placed by the State for purposes of care, protection, or treatment, to have all aspects of that placement regularly evaluated.

Article 26: The right to benefit from social security.

Article 27: The right to a standard of living adequate for her/his physical, mental, spiritual, moral, and social development.

Article 28: The right to education, including free primary education. Discipline to be consistent with a child's human dignity.

Article 29: The right to an education that prepares her/him for an active, responsible life as an adult in a free society which respects others and the environment.

Article 30: The right, if a member of a minority community or indigenous people, to enjoy her/his own culture, to practise her/his own religion, and to use her/his own language.

Article 31: The right to rest and leisure, to engage in play, and to participate in recreational, cultural, and artistic activities.

Article 32: The right to protection from economic exploitation and work that is hazardous, interferes with her/his education, or harms her/his

health or physical, mental, spiritual, moral, and social development.

Article 33: The right to protection from narcotic drugs and from being involved in their production or distribution.

Article 34: The right to protection from sexual exploitation and abuse.

Article 35: The right to protection from being abducted, sold, or trafficked.

Article 36: The right to protection from all other forms of exploitation.

Article 37: The right not to be subjected to torture or degrading treatment. If detained, not to be kept with adults, sentenced to death, nor imprisoned for life without the possibility of release. The right to legal assistance and contact with family.

Article 38: The right, if below 15 years of age, not to be recruited into armed forces nor to engage in direct hostilities.

Article 39: The right, if the victim of armed conflict, torture, neglect, maltreatment, or exploitation, to receive appropriate treatment for her/his physical and psychological recovery and reintegration into society.

Article 40: The right, if accused or guilty of committing an offense, to age-appropriate treatment likely to promote her/his sense of dignity and worth and her/his reintegration as a constructive member of society.

Article 42: The right to be informed of these principles and provisions by the state in which s/he lives.

Note: The Convention has 54 Articles in all. Articles 41 and 43 to 54 are concerned with its implementation and entry into force.

How to Use the Index

This general index is a key to all of the material in volumes 1 to 15 of *Childcraft*. The thousands of pages in *Childcraft* are filled with information on many subjects, in both text and pictures. Often, different aspects of a subject are covered in more than one volume. Although each volume has its own index, this general index is the only place to learn where in *Childcraft* you can find all the information on a subject.

The illustration on the opposite page shows the special features used in the general index and in the individual volume indexes. To make the best use of the indexes, you should be aware of these features.

An entry is in dark type. It can be the name of a person (**Daimler, Gottlieb**), a place (**Damascus**), a thing (**dandelion**), or a general topic. Many entries are subdivided to help you locate quickly the exact information you are looking for. One feature especially helpful for children is the use of an identifier in brackets after many of the entries, such as **date** (fruit). One entry that parents and teachers will find particularly helpful is **activities**. It lists all of the Try This! projects, games, and exercises in the set, grouping them under several broad subheadings that correspond

roughly to a breakdown by volume. This entry is found only in this volume and not in the individual indexes.

Cross-references guide you to additional headings and preferred headings. For example, if you are looking for information about day and night, the cross-reference *see also* **night, poems about,** tells you to look under that heading also. If you are looking for information about Leonardo da Vinci, the cross-reference **da Vinci, Leonardo,** *see* **Leonardo da Vinci** tells you where to look for the information.

The entries are arranged in alphabetical order. Some entries are inverted (**EDSA Revolution, Anniversary of**), so that the key portion of the entry is alphabetized.

The numbers following an entry or subentry (**15**/120) give the volume number in dark type and the page number or numbers in ordinary type. When there are references to more than one volume, the volumes are listed in numerical order.

If there is information in both words and pictures, the words *(with pictures)* appear after the page number or numbers. If the reference is to a picture only, the word *(picture)* appears after the volume and page number or numbers.

D

d (letter), rhyme about, 1/55

daddy longlegs, 4/137

dahlia, 4/8 *(picture)*

Daimler, Gottlieb (inventor), **9**/53

daisy, 5/160 *(with picture)*

dam, 6/95

  energy from, **8**/81

  of beaver, **4**/41 *(with picture)*

Damascus (Syria), **14**/93 *(picture)*

dance, 3/178-183 *(with pictures)*

  American Indian, **14**/109 *(picture)*,
    14/130 *(with picture)*

  Scottish, **14**/115 *(with picture)*

  stories about

    Cinderella, **2**/60-73

    Compae Rabbit's Ride, **2**/124-129

dandelion, 5/23 *(picture),* **5**/119
  (picture), **5**/162 *(with picture)*

dark nebula, 7/120 *(with picture)*

date (fruit), **5**/94 *(with picture)*

date bar (food), **12**/76-77 *(with
  pictures)*

da Vinci, Leonardo, *see* **Leonardo
  da Vinci**

dawdling, by child, 15/55

day and night, 6/11

  on Earth, **7**/18-19 *(with pictures),*
    7/72

  on Jupiter, **7**/80

  on Mars, **7**/74

  on Mercury, **7**/67

  on moon, **7**/57

  on Neptune, **7**/87

  on Pluto, **7**/88

  on Saturn, **7**/82

  on Uranus, **7**/84

  on Venus, **7**/71

  see also **night, poems about**

day care, 15/91-93 *(with picture)*

Daylight Savings Time (McGinley),
  1/83

Day-of-the-Dead festival, 14/162-
  163 *(with pictures)*

days of the week, poems about

  Monday's Child, 1/77

  Solomon Grundy, 1/76

  Wash on Monday, 1/76

Dead Sea (Asia), **6**/61 *(with picture)*

deafness, 11/78-79 *(with pictures),*
  12/138

Labels (left side):
- specific subject entry
- general subject entry
- subentry
- identifier
- cross-reference to preferred heading
- cross-reference to additional heading
- references listed in volume order

Labels (right side):
- volume number (in dark type) and page number reference to text only
- reference to picture(s) only
- volume 15 references are for parents and teachers
- reference to *both* text and picture(s)

A

B

b (letter), rhyme about, 1/54
Baa, Baa Black Sheep (Mother Goose), 1/105
Babbitt, Ellen C. (author)
How the Turtle Saved His Own Life, 2/93-95
baboon, 4/150-151 *(with pictures)*
baby, 11/96-99 *(with pictures)*, 11/116
before birth, 11/94-95 *(with pictures)*
birth of, see **birth**
body language of, 12/134
growth of, 11/102 *(with picture)*, 11/106, 11/107
head size of, 11/98, 11/106
mental retardation in, 15/112
newborn, 11/98-99 *(with pictures)*
physical disability in, 15/115
story about
Mother, Mother, I Want Another, 2/140-147
teeth of, 11/14
baby animal, see **animal**
Babylon (ancient city), 10/52-54 *(with pictures)*, 10/60
babysitter, 15/92-93
back (part of body), 11/87
Bacmeister, Rhoda W. (poet)
Stars, 1/44
bacteria, 4/164-165 *(with picture)*, 5/10 *(picture)*, 11/146-147, 11/178
Bad Kittens, The (Coatsworth), 1/119
Baikal, Lake (Russia), 6/91 *(with picture)*
bakery, 9/118-119
balance (sense), 11/61 *(with pictures)*, 11/68-69
balance scale (project), 10/167 *(with picture)*
Bali, 12/25 *(picture)*
dance of, 3/179 *(picture)*
ball (toy), 9/141 *(picture)*
ballad (song), 3/138
ballerina, 3/179-180 *(with picture)*
ballet, 3/179-180 *(with picture)*
balloon
hot-air, 8/96 *(with picture)*, 13/157
static electricity and (project), 8/163 *(with picture)*
weather, 6/147

bamboo, 4/20 *(with picture)*, 5/99 *(picture)*, 5/106-107 *(with picture)*, 5/118 *(picture)*
banana, 13/39 *(picture)*
band (music), 12/170 *(with picture)*
bandage, adhesive, 9/12 *(with picture)*
Banff National Park (Canada), 9/60 *(picture)*
Bangkok (Thailand), 12/61 *(picture)*
Bangladesh, 14/69
bank, of river, 6/85
banksia, 5/27 *(picture)*
bansuri (musical instrument), 3/127 *(with picture)*
baptism (ceremony), 12/23
Barber, Barber (Mother Goose), 1/23
barge child, 12/123 *(with picture)*
bar graph, 10/154-155 *(with picture)*
bark, on tree, 5/34
bark picture, 3/40-41
barley, 12/47
bar magnet, 8/39 *(picture)*
bar mitzvah (ceremony), 12/27 *(with picture)*, 14/103 *(with picture)*
barnacle, 4/10, 4/140-141 *(with picture)*
barometer, 6/150-151 *(with pictures)*
Barrie, James M. (playwright), 3/164-165 *(with picture)*
bartering, 13/78
basalt (mineral), 6/29
basil, 5/136 *(with picture)*
basketball, 12/91 *(picture)*
bass, black, 4/97 *(picture)*, 4/98
Bastille Day, 14/119-120 *(with pictures)*
bat (animal), 4/42-45 *(with pictures)*, 4/158, 5/27
Kitti's hog-nosed, 4/144 *(with picture)*
vampire, 4/43
Bathers at Asnières, The (Seurat), 3/68 *(with picture)*
bathing, 11/179 *(with picture)*, 11/180
batik (craft), 3/28-29 *(with pictures)*
bat mitzvah (ceremony), 12/27, 14/103
baton (music), 3/137 *(with picture)*

battery, 8/174-175 *(with pictures)*
battlement, 13/87, 13/90 *(with picture)*
Battle of Waterloo, 3/96 *(picture)*
bauxite (ore), 6/35 *(picture)*
bay, 6/83 *(with picture)*
beach, 6/80-81 *(with pictures)*, 13/171
beak, see **bill**
beam bridge, 9/162 *(with picture)*
bean
castor, 5/44 *(with picture)*
lima, 5/95 *(with picture)*
string, 5/138 *(picture)*
bear, 4/20, 4/24 *(picture)*
poems about
Fuzzy Wuzzy, 1/100
Grizzly Bear, 1/113
My Teddy Bear, 1/106
polar, 4/16 *(picture)*, 4/166
story about
Why Bear Has a Stumpy Tail, 2/106-107
beater brush, 9/23
beaver, 4/35 *(picture)*, 5/168 *(with picture)*
dam by, 4/41 *(with picture)*
bed, river, 6/85
bedtime
poems about
Bedtime Prayer, A, 1/47
Diddle, Diddle, Dumpling, 1/43
Down with the Lambs, 1/45
Early to Bed and Early to Rise, 1/45
Hippity Hop to Bed, 1/45
Jeremiah Obediah, 1/42
Now I Lay Me Down to Sleep, 1/47
Wee Willie Winkie, 1/42
story about
Mother, Mother, I Want Another, 2/140-147
Bedtime Prayer, A (poem), 1/47
bee, 5/27 *(picture)*
and flower markings, 8/133 *(with picture)*
honey, 4/134 *(with pictures)*
poem about
Bees, 1/117
beehive, 5/103 *(picture)*
beeper, see **pager**
Bees (Prelutsky), 1/117
beet, 5/99 *(picture)*, 12/53
beetle, 4/25 *(picture)*, 4/127 *(picture)*, 4/164

C

c (letter), rhyme about, **1**/55
Cabana, Robert D. (astronaut), **7**/181 *(picture)*
cabbage, 5/99 *(picture)*, **12**/53
caber-throwing contest, 14/115 *(with picture)*
cable-stayed bridge, 9/162 *(with pictures)*
cable television, 9/89 *(with picture)*
cactus, 5/13 *(picture)*, **5**/78-79 *(with pictures)*, **5**/127 *(picture)*, **5**/170
  barrel, **5**/78
  candelabra, **5**/79 *(picture)*
  pincushion, **5**/79 *(pictures)*
  prickly pear, **5**/131 *(picture)*
  saguaro, **5**/34 *(picture)*
CAD, *see* **computer-aided design**
caecilian, 4/89 *(with picture)*
Caesar, Julius (Roman emperor), **14**/111 *(with picture)*
calcium, in diet, 11/159
calculator (machine), **8**/179, **9**/35 *(with picture)*, **10**/109 *(picture)*, **10**/123-125 *(with pictures)*
  see also **abacus**
calendar, 14/14-19 *(with pictures)*
  April Fool's Day and, **14**/74
  as learning tool, **15**/72
  Chinese, **14**/17 *(with picture)*, **14**/42, **14**/101, **14**/145
  Christian, **14**/18
  Hebrew, **14**/18, **14**/103, **14**/141, **14**/177
  Islamic, **14**/19, **14**/30
  Stonehenge as, **10**/29
California (U.S.A.), **6**/29, **6**/165 *(with picture)*
caller ID, 9/101 *(with picture)*
Cambodia, 13/124 *(picture)*
camel, 4/17 *(picture)*, **12**/24 *(picture)*, **12**/34 *(picture)*, **12**/51, **12**/143 *(picture)*, **13**/48-49 *(with picture)*
camellia, 5/160
camera, 8/126-127 *(with pictures)*
  digital, **9**/11 *(picture)*
  television, **9**/88-89
Cameron, Ann (author)
  Pudding Like a Night on the Sea, The, **2**/166-177

camouflage, 4/148-149 *(with pictures)*
Canada, 12/129 *(picture)*, **12**/178, **13**/16, **14**/45, **14**/86, **14**/94, **14**/115
  ice hockey in, **12**/91
  sleds in, **13**/42 *(with picture)*
  special days in
    Canada Day, **14**/114 *(with picture)*
    Christmas, **14**/180
    Father's Day, **14**/104-105
    Remembrance Day, **14**/166 *(with pictures)*
    Thanksgiving, **14**/168, **14**/169
    Victoria Day, **14**/92
  see also **Inuit**
Canada Day, 14/114 *(with picture)*
canal, 13/100-101 *(with pictures)*
Cancer (constellation), **7**/110 *(with picture)*
candle, 12/24 *(picture)*, **12**/26 *(with pictures)*
  burning of, **8**/72 *(with picture)*
Cannon, Annie Jump (astronomer), **7**/157 *(with picture)*
cannonball tree, 5/75 *(picture)*
canoe, 13/45
can opener, 9/148 *(picture)*
Canopus (star), **7**/116
canopy (forest), **5**/74-75 *(with picture)*
cantilever bridge, 9/162 *(with picture)*
canyon, 6/61 *(picture)*
Canyon de Chelly (U.S.A.), **6**/61 *(picture)*
Cape Town (South Africa), **13**/15
car, 13/40-41 *(with pictures)*
  designing, **9**/82-83 *(with pictures)*
  gears in, **8**/24-25
  inertia and, **8**/30-31
  parts of, **9**/54-55 *(with pictures)*
  road signs, **12**/143-145 *(with pictures)*
  robot in manufacturing, **9**/174-175 *(with picture)*
  toy, **12**/102 *(picture)*
  travelling by, with children, **15**/98-99 *(with picture)*
caravan, 13/49 *(with picture)*
carbohydrate, 11/158, **11**/159
carbon, in telephone, 9/100 *(with picture)*

carbon dioxide, 4/18, **5**/112 *(with picture)*, **6**/169
  in air, **7**/73
  in bread, **9**/119
carbon monoxide detector, 15/61
careers
  animal-related, **4**/182-183 *(with pictures)*
  conservation, **6**/179-181 *(with pictures)*
  construction, **9**/156-157 *(with picture)*
  earth study, **6**/42-45 *(with pictures)*, **6**/59
  engineering, *see* **engineer**
  manufacturing, **9**/146-147 *(with pictures)*
  mapmaking, **13**/158-159 *(with pictures)*
  ocean study, **6**/100-101 *(with pictures)*
  physical science, **8**/180-183 *(with pictures)*
  plant-related, **5**/120-123 *(with pictures)*
  space, **7**/172-173 *(with picture)*
  travel-related, **13**/178-183 *(with pictures)*
  weather study, **6**/146-147 *(with pictures)*
caribou, 4/160-161 *(with picture)*, **12**/62 *(picture)*
Caring (Madkour), **3**/52-53 *(with picture)*
Carle, Eric (artist), **3**/18-19 *(with pictures)*
carnivore, 4/13
carol (song), **14**/179
carp, 3/11, **4**/96 *(with picture)*, **14**/88-91 *(with pictures)*
carpenter, 9/156 *(with picture)*
carpet, 12/38 *(picture)*, **12**/126 *(with picture)*
Carroll, Lewis (author)
  Jabberwocky, **1**/152
  Through the Looking Glass, **5**/144-149 *(with pictures)*
carrot, 5/97 *(with picture)*, **5**/99 *(picture)*, **5**/138 *(picture)*, **12**/53
cartilage, 11/102
cartographer, 13/159 *(with picture)*
cartoon, 12/135 *(picture)*

D

d (letter), rhyme about, 1/55
daddy longlegs, 4/137
dahlia, 4/8 *(picture)*
Dai, 5/107 *(with picture)*
Daimler, Gottlieb (inventor), 9/53
daisy, 5/160 *(with picture)*
dam, 6/95
  energy from, 8/81
  of beaver, 4/41 *(with picture)*
Damascus (Syria), 14/93 *(picture)*
dance, 3/178-183 *(with pictures)*
  American Indian, 14/109 *(picture)*,
    14/130 *(with picture)*
  Scottish, 14/115 *(with picture)*
  stories about
    Cinderella, 2/60-73
    Compae Rabbit's Ride, 2/124-129
dandelion, 5/23 *(picture)*, 5/119
  (picture), 5/162 *(with picture)*
dark nebula, 7/120 *(with picture)*
date (fruit), 5/94 *(with picture)*
date bar (food), 12/76-77 *(with*
  pictures)
da Vinci, Leonardo, see
  Leonardo da Vinci
dawdling, by child, 15/55
day and night, 6/11
  on Earth, 7/18-19 *(with pictures)*,
    7/72
  on Jupiter, 7/80
  on Mars, 7/74
  on Mercury, 7/67
  on moon, 7/57
  on Neptune, 7/87
  on Pluto, 7/88
  on Saturn, 7/82
  on Uranus, 7/84
  on Venus, 7/71
  see also **night, poems about**
day care, 15/91-93 *(with picture)*
Daylight Saving Time (McGinley),
  1/83
Day-of-the-Dead festival,
  14/162-163 *(with pictures)*
days of the week, poems about
  Monday's Child, 1/77
  Solomon Grundy, 1/76
  Wash on Monday, 1/76
Dead Sea (Asia), 6/61 *(with picture)*
deafness, 11/78-79 *(with pictures)*,
  12/138

death, 11/140-141 *(with pictures)*
  explaining to child, 15/102-103
    (with picture)
decagon (shape), 10/37 *(picture)*
December, 14/170-181 *(with*
  pictures)
  birthdays in, 14/172-173 *(with*
    pictures)
  birthstone for, 6/33 *(picture)*
decibel, 8/157
decomposer, in food chain,
  4/163
deer, 4/155, 4/179
Degas, Edgar (artist), 3/60
degree (distance), 13/153
Deimos (moon), 7/60, 7/75
deinotherium (extinct animal),
  4/172-173 *(with picture)*
de la Mare, Walter (poet)
  Somewhere, 13/177
Delhi (India), 13/13
della Porta, Gianbattista
  (mathematician), 10/149
delphinium (plant), 5/142 *(picture)*
delta, 6/86 *(with picture)*
Delta rocket, 9/78 *(picture)*
Denmark, 6/178, 14/106
  story from
    Emperor's New Clothes, The, 2/36-
    47
dentist, 11/174-175 *(with picture)*,
  15/59
Denver (U.S.A.), 6/63 *(picture)*
depth, of shape, 10/42 *(with*
  picture)
Derrah (game), 12/106-107 *(with*
  pictures)
desert, 4/70-71 *(with pictures)*,
  6/64-67 *(with pictures)*, 6/99,
  6/154 *(picture)*
  clothing for, 13/74-75 *(with picture)*
  plants of, 5/41 *(with picture)*, 5/76-
    79 *(with pictures)*
  travel in, 13/48-49 *(with picture)*
design, 9/150 *(with picture)*
  see also **computer-aided
    design; engineer**
dessert, 12/58-59 *(with pictures)*
development, of land, 6/166 *(with*
  picture)
Devil's Postpile (U.S.A.), 6/29
diameter, of circle, 10/27 *(with*
  picture)
diamond (gem), 6/32-33 *(with*
  pictures)
Diana (goddess), 7/42

diaphragm (part of body), 11/51
  (with picture)
diaphragm (telephone), 9/100-101
  (with picture)
dice, 10/42 *(picture)*, 10/110 *(with*
  picture)
  chance in rolling, 10/134-135 *(with*
    picture)
Dickson, Earle (inventor), 9/12
Diddle, Diddle, Dumpling (Mother
  Goose), 1/43
dIet, see **food**
differences, individual, see
  uniqueness; sex differences
digestion, by plant, 5/48-49
digital camera, 9/11 *(picture)*
digital code, 9/30-31, 9/36-39
  (with picture), 9/106
digitalis, 5/117
digital thermometer, 9/14-15
  (with picture)
digital video disc, 9/40 *(with*
  picture)
Diller, a Dollar, A (Mother Goose),
  1/81
Dimetrodon (ancient lizardlike
  animal), 6/37 *(picture)*
dinosaur, 4/168-170 *(with pictures)*,
  6/36 *(with picture)*
Dinosaur National Monument
  (U.S.A.), 13/109 *(with picture)*
directions
  on compass, 13/146
  on map, 13/136-137 *(with picture)*
director (theatre), 3/152-153
disability
  learning, 15/109-111 *(with picture)*
  physical, 9/177 *(with picture)*,
    11/130-131 *(with picture)*,
    15/115-116 *(with picture)*
disabled, see **disability**
discipline, for children, 15/56-58
  (with picture), 15/113-115
disease, see **illness**
distance, on map, 13/140-141
  (with picture)
Divali (festival), 14/154-155 *(with*
  pictures)
division, 10/126-129 *(with pictures)*
division facts, 10/129
doctor, 11/153-155 *(with pictures)*
Doctor Foster Went to Gloucester
  (Mother Goose), 1/36
dodder plant, 5/47 *(with picture)*
dodo (bird), 4/166-167 *(with picture)*

E

F

f (letter), rhyme about, 1/56
fables, 1/169
Ant and the Dove, The, 1/174
Blind Men and the Elephant, The,
   11/30-35 *(with pictures)*
Crow and the Jug, The, 1/172
Dog and the Bone, The, 1/175
Hare and the Tortoise, The, 1/173
How Chameleon Became a Teacher,
   1/176-181
Lion and the Mouse, The, 1/171
fabric, 9/134-135 *(with pictures),*
   9/144-145 *(with pictures)*
in crafts, 3/24-31 *(with pictures)*
face, 11/10-11 *(with pictures)*
bones of, 11/40 *(with picture)*
two sides of, 11/12-13 *(with
   pictures)*
factory
assembly line in, 9/83 *(with
   pictures),* 9/146 *(with pictures)*
workers in, 9/146-147 *(with
   pictures)*
Fahrenheit (temperature), 9/15
failure, in school, 15/79-80
fairy, see **elves and fairies,
   stories about**
fairy tales, 2/11
Cinderella, 2/60-73
Emperor's New Clothes, The, 2/36-
   47
Jack and the Beanstalk, 2/12-21
Old Woman and Her Dumpling, The,
   2/48-57
Prince and the Orphan, The,
   2/74-87
Shoemaker and the Elves, The,
   2/24-33
falcon, peregrine, 4/11, 4/59 *(with
   picture)*
falls, poems about
Humpty Dumpty, 1/22
Ring-a-Ring o' Roses, 1/139
family, 12/9-13 *(with pictures)*
activities, 12/20-25 *(with
   pictures)*
drawing members of (project),
   11/131 *(with picture)*
members looking alike, 11/100-
   101 *(with picture)*
mental retardation and, 15/114
names, 12/14-17 *(with pictures)*
poems about

My Little Golden Sister, 1/16
Peter, Peter, Pumpkin-Eater, 1/25
Rock-a-Bye Baby, 1/40
Two Little Sisters, 1/17
Walking, 1/16
problems in, 15/80
stories about
Cinderella, 2/60-73
Jack and the Beanstalk, 2/12-21
Mother, Mother, I Want Another,
   2/140-147
Pudding Like a Night on the Sea,
   The, 2/166-177
Thousand Pails of Water, A, 2/181-
   189
traditions, 12/22-25 *(with pictures)*
types of, 11/108-109 *(with
   pictures)*
work sharing in, 12/166-167 *(with
   pictures)*
family day care, 15/92
family tree, 11/111-113 *(with
   picture)*
fan (machine), 9/11 *(picture),* 9/42
   (picture)
hairdryer, 9/25 *(with picture)*
vacuum cleaner, 9/23 *(with picture)*
Farjeon, Eleanor (poet)
Kitten, A, 1/118
Moon-Come-Out, 1/40
farmer, 4/183
farming, 13/78 *(with picture)*
fasting, 14/12, 14/30-31, 14/51,
   14/54, 14/75
fat, in diet, 11/158, 11/160,
   11/162-163 *(picture),* 11/169
father, 11/108, 12/10, 12/12,
   14/104-105 *(with picture)*
baby's birth and, 11/92
family tree and, 11/111 *(with
   picture)*
genes from, 11/100-101 *(with
   pictures)*
growing child and, 11/116-117
see also **parent**
Father Christmas, 14/180,
   14/181
Father's Day, 14/104-105 *(with
   picture)*
fault-block mountain, 6/53 *(with
   picture)*
fax machine, 9/98 *(with picture)*
fear
in preschool child, 15/55-56
of death, 15/103
unrealistic, 15/105-106, 15/108

feather, 4/50, 4/56-57 *(with
   pictures)*
February, 14/38-55 *(with pictures)*
birthdays in, 14/40-41 *(with
   pictures)*
birthstone for, 6/33 *(picture)*
feelings, see **thoughts and
   feelings**
feet, see **foot**
fern, 5/15 *(with picture),* 5/153 *(with
   picture)*
ostrich plume, 4/8 *(picture)*
Ferris wheel, 10/26 *(with picture)*
ferry, 13/45
fibre, 5/108
natural, 9/134-135 *(with pictures),*
   9/145 *(picture)*
synthetic, 9/144-145 *(with pictures)*
fibreglass, 9/83, 9/163
fibre-optic cable, 8/136-137 *(with
   picture)*
Field, Rachel (poet)
If Once You Have Slept on an Island,
   1/86
figurehead (carving), 3/10 *(with
   picture)*
Fiji, 12/21 *(picture),* 12/136 *(picture)*
filament, 8/166-167 *(with pictures)*
film (camera), 8/127 *(with picture)*
finger, 11/22
bones of, 11/40 *(with picture),*
   11/42 *(picture)*
touch, sense of, 11/87
fingernail, 11/24-25 *(with picture)*
finger painting, 3/43, 3/65 *(with
   picture)*
fingerprint, 11/26-27 *(with
   pictures),* 11/97, 11/120-121
finger spelling, 11/79 *(with picture)*
Finland, 13/43, 14/107
music in, 3/117 *(picture)*
fins, 4/90
fir, Douglas, 5/38 *(picture)*
fire
energy from, 8/72-73 *(with
   pictures),* 8/131 *(picture)*
first use of (story), 8/104-111
   (with pictures)
forest, 5/176-177 *(with pictures)*
grassland, 5/60
Fire Bringer, The (story), 8/104-111
   (with pictures)
fire drill, 15/60
firefighter, 5/177 *(with picture)*
firefly, 4/152
fire lily, 5/86 *(picture)*
fire safety, 11/181

G

g (letter), rhyme about, **1**/56
Ga (people), **14**/132-133 *(with picture)*
Gabo, Naum (sculptor), **3**/98 *(with picture)*
gagaku orchestra, 3/111
Gagarin, Yuri (cosmonaut), **7**/164 *(with picture)*
galaxy, 7/125, **7**/130-131 *(with pictures)*
    see also **Milky Way Galaxy**
gale, 6/119 *(pictures)*
Galileo (scientist), **7**/111-115 *(with picture)*
Galileo (space probe), **7**/81, **7**/182 *(picture)*
game (recreation), **12**/79-89 *(with pictures)*, **12**/106-109 *(with pictures)*
    learning with, **12**/114-115 *(with pictures)*
    see also **activities; play** (recreation); **sports**
gamelan orchestra, 3/111 *(with picture)*
game warden, 4/183
Gandhi, Mohandas Karamchand (Indian leader), **14**/151 *(with picture)*
Ganges River (India), **12**/25, **13**/125 *(with picture)*
Ganymede (moon), **7**/61 *(with picture)*
garage-door opener, 9/93, **9**/109 *(picture)*
garden, 5/125-157 *(with pictures)*
    butterfly, **5**/150-151 *(with pictures)*
    hanging, **5**/29
    herb, **5**/136-137 *(with pictures)*
    indoor, **5**/126-129 *(with pictures)*
    outdoor, **5**/130-135 *(with pictures)*
    rock, **5**/152-153 *(with pictures)*
    scent, **5**/154-155 *(with pictures)*
gardener, 5/122 *(with picture)*
Gardner, John (poet)
    Lizard, The, **1**/110
garlic, 5/33
garnet, 6/33 *(picture)*
gas, 6/108-109, **8**/53, **8**/58-63 *(with pictures)*
    evaporation and, **8**/88 *(with picture)*

formation of sun from, **7**/13 *(with picture)*
    in car engine, **9**/57
    in comet, **7**/104
    in refrigerator, **9**/16-17 *(with picture)*
    on Venus, **7**/70
gatehouse, 13/87, **13**/91 *(with picture)*
gear, 8/24-25 *(with pictures)*
    in bicycle, **9**/51 *(with pictures)*
    in escalator, **9**/48-49 *(picture)*
gear lever, 9/55 *(with picture)*
gecko, 4/77 *(picture)*
    Tokay, **4**/78 *(picture)*
    West Indian, **4**/144 *(with picture)*
gem, 6/32-33 *(with pictures)*
Gemini (constellation), **7**/111 *(with picture)*
gene, 11/100-101 *(with picture)*
generator, 8/68, **8**/75, **8**/170-171 *(with picture)*
    car, **9**/55 *(with picture)*
geochemist (scientist), **6**/45 *(with picture)*
geodesic dome, 13/114 *(with picture)*
geographer, 13/159
geologist (scientist), **6**/42-43 *(with pictures)*
    environmental, **6**/43 *(with picture)*
    mining, **6**/44
    petroleum, **6**/44 *(with picture)*
geology, 6/42-43 *(with pictures)*
Georgie Porgie (Mother Goose), **1**/17
geranium, 5/126 *(picture)*, **5**/131 *(with picture)*
germ (organism), **11**/50
    sickness from, **11**/146
    washing away, **11**/178-179
German (language), **10**/49
Germany, 6/92 *(picture)*, **12**/83, **12**/137 *(picture)*, **12**/167 *(picture)*, **14**/179, **14**/180
    barge children in, **12**/123 *(with picture)*
    castle in, **13**/93 *(with picture)*
    eating customs in, **12**/66 *(picture)*
    food in, **12**/47, **12**/69
    language in, **12**/133
    nursery rhyme from
        Here is the Family, **1**/134
    story from
        Shoemaker and the Elves, The, **2**/24-33

germination, 5/28-29 *(with pictures)*
geyser, 6/98-99 *(with picture)*
Ghana, 12/12 *(with picture)*, **14**/132-133 *(with picture)*
giant, stories about
    Glooscap and His People, **2**/130-137
    Jack and the Beanstalk, **2**/12-21
    Giant, The (Prokofiev), **3**/130
Giant's Causeway (Northern Ireland), **6**/28-29 *(with pictures)*
gift, story about
    Shoemaker and the Elves, The, **2**/24-33
Gilbert, Alice (poet)
    I Ate a Ton of Sugar, **1**/28
gills, 4/25, **4**/90
ginkgo, 5/15 *(with picture)*
giraffe, 4/34-35 *(picture)*
girl, 11/58-59 *(with picture)*, **11**/107
    maturation of, **15**/77, **15**/85, **15**/87 *(picture)*, **15**/90
    motor development of, **15**/68
    poems about
        Little Bo-Peep, **1**/27
        Little Miss Muffet, **1**/28
        Mary, Mary Quite Contrary, **1**/22
        Mary Had a Little Lamb, **1**/14
        Mary Had a Pretty Bird, **1**/95
        My Little Golden Sister, **1**/16
        Two Little Sisters, **1**/17
    social development of, **15**/65
    stories about
        Cinderella, **2**/60-73
        Prince and the Orphan, The, **2**/74-87
    see also **child; sister**
Girls' Festival, 14/60 *(with picture)*
Giza (Egypt), **13**/15 *(picture)*, **13**/103 *(with picture)*
Glacial Tarn (lake, U.S.A.), **6**/93 *(picture)*
glacier, 6/61, **6**/70-71 *(with picture)*, **6**/93
gladiolus, 5/143 *(with picture)*
gland
    animal, **4**/155
    human, **11**/106-107 *(with picture)*
glass, 9/136-137 *(with pictures)*
    in house, **9**/152
    see also **fibreglass**
glass blower, 9/137 *(picture)*
glasses, 11/72-73 *(with pictures)*
glass snake, 4/76 *(with picture)*
Glaubitz, Grace (poet)
    Walking, **1**/16

glazing, of pottery, **9**/133
Glenn, John (astronaut), **7**/164 *(with picture)*
globe, **13**/32-33 *(with picture),* **13**/148-149 *(with pictures)*
Glooscap and His People (story), **2**/130-137
glottis, **11**/75 *(picture)*
glove puppet, **3**/166-167 *(with picture),* **3**/170-171 *(with pictures)*
goat, **5**/169, **12**/51
  story about
    Three Billy Goats Gruff, The, **2**/97-99
Gobi Desert (Asia), **13**/13
goby, dwarf (fish), **4**/145 *(with picture)*
Goddard, Robert H. (scientist), **7**/158
godmother, story about
  Cinderella, **2**/60-73
gods and goddesses, see **mythology**
gold (metal), **6**/35 *(with picture),* **8**/53 *(with picture)*
goldfish, **4**/11, **4**/29 *(picture)*
golomyanka (fish), **6**/97
gong, **3**/114
gongo (drum), **12**/147 *(with picture)*
Good, Better, Best (poem), **1**/89
Good Friday, 14/78
good luck plant, **5**/32 *(with picture)*
Good Night (Fyleman), **1**/50
Good Sportsmanship (Armour), **1**/89
googol (number), **10**/106
goose, **4**/65, **4**/154 *(picture)*
gorilla, mountain, **5**/84
Go to Sleep (nursery rhyme), **1**/48
government buildings, **13**/94 *(with pictures)*
grading machine, **9**/171 *(with picture)*
graduation, **12**/22-23 *(with picture)*
Graham, Martha (dancer), **3**/180
Grahame, Kenneth (poet)
  Ducks' Ditty, **1**/127
grain, **6**/44 *(picture),* **12**/47 *(with picture)*
Grand Canyon (Arizona), **13**/119 *(with picture)*
grandfather, **11**/108, **11**/111 *(with picture),* **12**/10, **12**/12, **15**/63 *(picture)*
  as friend to child, **15**/62 *(with picture)*

death of, **15**/102-103
Father's Day and, **14**/105 *(with picture)*
learning from, **12**/117
Grandfather Frost (tradition), **14**/24 *(picture)*
grandmother, **11**/108, **11**/111 *(with picture),* **12**/10, **12**/12
  as friend to child, **15**/62
  death of, **15**/102-103
granite, **6**/23 *(with picture)*
grape, **5**/104 *(picture)*
graph, **10**/154-155 *(with pictures)*
graphite, **6**/26 *(picture)*
grass, **5**/33 *(with picture),* **5**/62-63 *(with pictures),* **5**/90-91 *(with pictures)*
  eel, **5**/53
  hairy spinifex, **5**/63 *(picture)*
  Indian, **5**/62 *(picture)*
  kangaroo, **5**/62 *(with picture)*
  Mitchell, **5**/62 *(with picture)*
  pampas, **5**/62 *(with picture)*
  quaking, **5**/62 *(picture)*
  rattlesnake, **5**/62 *(picture)*
grasshopper, **4**/15 *(picture),* **4**/124 *(with picture),* **4**/126-127 *(with picture),* **4**/148, **4**/152 *(picture)*
grassland, **5**/60-63 *(with pictures)*
gravity, **6**/13, **7**/41, **7**/57, **7**/86, **7**/124, **8**/41
  air and, **6**/105, **6**/109
  earth's shape and, **6**/16 *(with pictures)*
  orbiting and, **8**/46-47 *(with pictures)*
  satellite and, **8**/44-45
grease paint, **3**/163
Great Barrier Reef (Australia), **13**/25, **13**/120 *(with picture)*
Great Bear (constellation), see **Ursa Major**
Great Britain, see **United Kingdom**
Great Lakes (North America), **6**/96
Great Mosque (Mecca), **13**/124-125 *(with picture)*
Great Nebula, 7/120 *(picture)*
Great Plains (North America), **6**/63
Great Red Spot (Jupiter), **7**/81 *(with picture)*
Great Sphinx, 3/90 *(with picture)*
Great Victoria Desert (Australia), **13**/25

Great Wall of China, 13/13, **13**/105 *(with picture)*
Great Zimbabwe (ancient city, Africa), **13**/106 *(picture)*
grebe, **5**/64
  eared, **4**/64 *(picture)*
Greece, 12/79, **12**/137 *(picture),* **13**/46 *(picture)*
  Easter in, **14**/16 *(picture)*
  food in, **12**/51, **12**/52 *(picture)*
  Independence Day in, **14**/69 *(with picture)*
  Parthenon in, **13**/107 *(with picture)*
Greece, ancient, 12/27, **12**/79, **12**/101 *(picture)*
  numbers in, **10**/61 *(with picture)*
  theatre in, **3**/147
  see also **Greek mythology**
Greek mythology
  star, **7**/110-111 *(with pictures)*
  sun, **7**/30
green (colour), **8**/128, **8**/131, **9**/90, **14**/61
greenhouse effect, **6**/168-169 *(with pictures)*
Greenpeace, 6/180
Greenwich (England), **13**/152
grieving, **11**/141 *(with picture)*
  see also **mourning**
grill (appliance), **9**/43 *(picture)*
Grimm brothers (authors), **2**/22-23
  Shoemaker and the Elves, The, **2**/24-33
Grizzly Bear (Austin), **1**/113
grocery trolley, **9**/47 *(picture)*
Groovin' High (Ringgold), **3**/27
grouper, spotted, **4**/100 *(with picture)*
grown-up, learning from, **12**/117
growth, human, **11**/90-107 *(with pictures)*
  after birth, **11**/99, **11**/102 *(with pictures)*
  before birth, **11**/92-94 *(with pictures)*
  boy-girl differences, **11**/59
  growing world and, **11**/116-117 *(with pictures)*
  of school-age child, **15**/69, **15**/85-90 *(with pictures)*
growth chart, **11**/105 *(with picture),* **15**/85
growth hormone, **11**/107, **15**/90

H

I

i (letter), rhyme about, 1/57
I Ate a Ton of Sugar (Gilbert),
  1/28
ibex, Pyrenean, 4/179 *(picture)*
ice, 8/88 *(with picture)*
  crystals of, in clouds, 6/124-125
  in Antarctica, 13/20-21
  in glacier, 6/70-71 *(with picture)*
  poem about
    Ice, 1/83
  travel on, 13/42-43 *(with pictures)*
  see also hail; snow
Ice (Aldis), 1/83
iceberg, 6/71
ice cream, 9/124-125 *(with
  pictures),* 14/120 *(with pictures)*
Iceland, 6/69, 14/89
  volcanoes of, 6/54 *(picture),* 6/56-
  57 *(with pictures)*
ichthyologist (scientist), 4/183
identical twins, 11/101 *(with
  picture)*
I Eat My Peas with Honey
  (poem), 1/33
If All the World Were Paper
  (Mother Goose), 1/32
*If Once You Have Slept on an
  Island* (Field), 1/86
igneous rock, 6/23 *(with picture)*
ignition, car, 9/56 *(with picture)*
Iguaçu Falls (South America),
  13/19, 13/117 *(with picture),*
  13/162 *(picture)*
iguana, 4/69 *(picture)*
I Had a Little Hobby Horse
  (Mother Goose), 1/104
I Had a Little Pig (poem), 1/113
illness, 11/146-147
  height and, 15/90
  insects and, 4/130-131 *(with
    pictures)*
  lack of sleep and, 11/177
  of school-age child, 15/75-76
  pain and, 11/152-153 *(with
    pictures)*
  see also injury *and specific illnesses*
I Love You, I Love You (poem),
  1/15
imagination, in preschool
  children, 15/52-53

I Met a Man (poem), 1/24
immunization, 11/157, 15/74
impressionism, 3/48 *(with picture),*
  3/54-55 *(with pictures),* 3/60-61
  (with pictures), 3/67
Inca (people), 13/104
incense, 14/117
inch, 10/163
inch-pound system, 10/163
inclined plane, 8/14-15 *(with
  picture),* 8/19
Independence Day
  Bolívar's birthday, 14/121 *(with
    picture)*
  in Brazil, 14/139 *(with picture)*
  in Equatorial Guinea, 14/69
  in Greece, 14/69 *(with picture)*
  in India, 14/35
  in Indonesia, 14/129
  in Mauritius, 14/69
  in Mexico, 14/142-143 *(with
    picture)*
  in U.S.A., 14/116 *(with picture)*
India, 12/24, 12/31 *(picture),* 12/33
  (picture), 12/99, 12/178, 13/95
  (picture), 13/100
  arts of
    dance, 3/179 *(picture),* 3/182-183
      (with pictures)
    kites, 12/104
    music, 3/125 *(with picture),* 3/127
      (with picture)
    theatre, 3/147 *(with picture)*
  clothes in, 13/74 *(picture)*
  food in, 12/39 *(picture),* 12/47,
    12/50
  forest in, 5/159 *(picture)*
  funeral in, 12/25
  games in, 12/81 *(picture),* 12/86
    (with picture)
  Ganges River in, 13/125 *(with
    picture)*
  language of, 12/131 *(picture)*
  proverb from, 1/183
  school in, 12/115 *(picture),* 12/118
    (picture), 12/124 *(picture)*
  special days in
    Buddha's birthday, 14/75
    Divali, 14/154-155 *(with pictures)*
    Gandhi's birthday, 14/151 *(with
      picture)*
    New Year, 14/26
  star myth from, 7/112 *(with
    picture),* 7/141

stories from
    Blind Men and the Elephant, The,
      11/30-35
    How the Turtle Saved His Own Life,
      2/93-95
  transportation in, 13/37 *(with
    picture)*
  see also Taj Mahal
Indian Ocean, 6/74 *(with picture)*
Indian pipe plant, 5/13 *(with
  picture)*
Indians, American, 14/109
  (picture), 14/169 *(with picture)*
  ceremonies of, 12/26
  clothes of, 12/28 *(picture)*
  corn legend of, 5/92-93 *(with
    pictures)*
  dances, 3/178 *(with picture)*
  moon myth of, 7/43-44 *(with
    picture)*
  poems of
    Away in the East, 1/46
    By the Sandy Water, 1/85
    This Land, 1/86
  sign language of, 12/139 *(with
    pictures)*
  sky myth of, 7/141 *(with picture)*
  song of, 1/40
  story from
    Glooscap and His People, 2/130-
      137
  sun myth of, 7/28-29 *(with picture)*
  totem poles of, 3/94-95 *(with
    pictures)*
  tribal name of, 12/26
  weaving by, 12/38 *(picture)*
  see also Inuit *and specific tribes*
Indonesia, 12/53, 12/59 *(picture)*
  game from, 12/89 *(with picture)*
  Independence Day in, 14/129 *(with
    picture)*
  music in, 3/111 *(with picture)*
industry, and pollution, 6/177
  (with picture)
inertia, 8/30-31 *(with pictures)*
infant, *see* baby
infinite number, 10/107
influenza, *see* flu
information, and brain, 11/62-63
  (with picture)
infrared rays, 8/133, 9/15, 9/31,
  9/93
ingot, 9/139
injection (medicine), 11/157,
  11/175

J

j (letter), rhyme about, 1/57
Jabberwocky (Carroll), 1/152
jack (machine), 8/19 *(picture)*
Jack and the Beanstalk (story), 2/12-21
jacks (game), 12/86
Jackson, Leroy F. (poet)
    Hippity Hop to Bed, 1/45
Jack Sprat (Mother Goose), 1/30
jaguar, story about
    Clever Frog, 2/118-123
Jains (people), 12/57
Jakarta (Indonesia), 14/129
January, 14/20-37 *(with pictures)*
    birthdays in, 14/22-23 *(with pictures)*
    birthstone for, 6/33 *(picture)*
Janus (god), 14/21 *(with picture)*
Japan, 12/30 *(picture)*, 12/135 *(picture)*, 13/13, 13/66-68, 14/152
    Akashi Kaikyo Bridge in, 13/98 *(with picture)*
    arts of
        kitemaking, 3/11 *(with picture)*
        music, 3/111, 3/119 *(picture)*
        paper crafts, 3/14-15 *(with pictures)*, 3/22-23 *(with pictures)*
        puppets, 3/168-169 *(with picture)*
        theatre, 3/149 *(with picture)*
    castles in, 13/92 *(with picture)*
    eating customs in, 12/67 *(with picture)*
    etiquette in, 12/156 *(with picture)*
    family in, 12/12, 12/20 *(picture)*, 12/23 *(with picture)*
    food in, 12/55 *(with picture)*, 12/63 *(with picture)*
    games in, 12/89, 12/91
    holidays in, 12/97 *(with picture)*
    national parks in, 13/109 *(with picture)*, 13/121 *(with picture)*
    poems from
        haiku, 1/164-165
        Little Duck, the, 1/126
        Lost Snowflake, A, 1/37

Prancing Pony, The, 1/94
Song of the Frog, The, 1/49
solar myth from, 7/31 *(with picture)*
special days in
    Children's Day, 14/89 *(with picture)*
    doll festivals, 14/60 *(with pictures)*
    New Year's Day, 14/26 *(with picture)*
    Seven-Five-Three, 14/165 *(with picture)*
    Star Festival, 14/126-128 *(with pictures)*
    star mythology of, 14/126-127 *(with picture)*
stories from
    Old Woman and Her Dumpling, The, 2/48-57
    Thousand Pails of Water, A, 2/181-189
wedding in, 12/24 *(with picture)*
see also **Tokyo**
Japanese (language), 10/49, 12/131 *(picture)*, 13/30-31
Japanese garden, 5/156 *(picture)*
jasmine, 5/118 *(picture)*
Java, 14/129
jawan (soldier), 14/35
jawfish, 4/98 *(with picture)*
jellyfish, 4/108, 4/122-123 *(with pictures)*
Jemison, Mae Carol (astronaut), 7/165 *(with picture)*
Jeremiah Obediah (Mother Goose), 1/42
Jerusalem, 13/122-123 *(with pictures)*
Jesus Christ, 14/108
    Easter and, 14/178-179 *(with pictures)*
    Feast of Epiphany and, 14/29
jet plane, 9/74-75 *(with pictures)*, 9/80 *(picture)*
jet stream, 6/115
jewellery, 12/30 *(picture)*, 12/32-33 *(with pictures)*
    from plants, 5/119 *(with picture)*
    see also **necklace**

Jews, see **Judaism**
jicama (plant), 5/99 *(picture)*
job, see **careers**
joey (kangaroo), 4/36-37 *(with pictures)*
Johnson Space Center, 7/174
John the Baptist, St. (Christian saint), 14/108
joint (part of body), 11/42 *(with pictures)*
Joshua tree, 5/78 *(picture)*
Jōsō (poet)
    Little Duck, The, 1/126
Juárez, Benito (Mexican leader), 14/67
Judaism
    bar and bat mitzvah in, 12/27 *(with picture)*, 14/103 *(with picture)*
    diet and, 12/57
    places of worship for, 13/122-123 *(with picture)*
    special days for
        Hanukkah, 14/176-177 *(with pictures)*
        Passover, 14/80-81 *(with pictures)*
        Rosh Ha-Shanah, 14/26, 14/140-141 *(with pictures)*
        Shavuot, 14/102-103 *(with pictures)*
        Yom Kippur, 14/140-141 *(with pictures)*
juice, 5/104
July, 14/110-121 *(with pictures)*
    birthdays in, 14/112-113 *(with pictures)*
    birthstone for, 6/33 *(picture)*
Jump or Jiggle (Beyer), 1/115
June, 14/96-109 *(with pictures)*
    birthdays in, 14/98-99 *(with pictures)*
    birthstone for, 6/33 *(picture)*
juniper, 5/70 *(picture)*
junk food, 11/168-169 *(with picture)*
Juno (goddess), 14/97 *(with picture)*
Jupiter (planet), 7/64 *(with picture)*, 7/81 *(with pictures)*, 7/91 *(with picture)*, 7/97, 7/145
    moons of, 7/60-61 *(with picture)*
jute, 9/135 *(picture)*

K

k (letter), rhyme about, 1/57
Kaaba (building, Saudi Arabia),
    13/124-125
Kabuki (theatre), 3/149 (with
    picture)
Kalahari Desert (Africa), 7/28,
    12/112 (picture)
Kalundborg (Denmark), 6/178
kangaroo, 4/10 (picture), 4/36-37
    (with pictures)
kantele (musical instrument),
    3/117 (picture)
karamu (ceremony), 14/182
    (picture)
Keller, Irene (poet)
    Thingumajigs, 1/90-91
kelp, 5/52 (picture)
Kennedy Space Center (Florida),
    7/179 (picture), 7/181 (picture)
Kenya, 12/28 (picture), 12/32-33,
    13/65, 13/119 (with picture)
Kepler, Johannes (scientist), 7/143
keratin (skin), 11/24
kerigami (craft), 3/22-23 (with
    pictures)
kettle drum, 3/115
key, 9/149 (picturc)
keyboard, 9/35 (picture)

keyboard instrument, 3/122
    (with picture)
keystone, 9/161 (with picture)
Keystone Canyon (Alaska), 13/39
    (picture)
Khafre (king of Egypt), 3/90
Khufu (king of Egypt), 3/90
kibbutz (community), 12/11 (with
    picture)
kidney, 11/56-57 (with pictures)
Kilimanjaro (mountain, Africa),
    13/15
kiln, 9/133
kilometre (measurement), 10/163
kilt, 14/115 (with picture)
kilt (clothes), 12/29 (picture)
kimono (clothes), 12/24 (picture),
    12/30 (picture), 14/164 (picture)
kinara (candleholder), 14/182 (with
    picture)
kindergarten, 15/54
king, 12/14, 12/179 (picture)
poems about
    Humpty Dumpty, 1/22
    Old King Cole, 1/20
    Sing a Song of Sixpence, 1/28
stories about
    Emperor's New Clothes, The, 2/36-
    47
    Prince and the Orphan, The, 2/74-
    87

King, Martin Luther, Jr. (civil
    rights leader), 14/36-37 (with
    pictures)
kingdom, 5/11
kingfisher (bird), 4/52 (picture)
kite, 3/11 (with picture), 8/67 (with
    picture), 8/68 (with picture),
    12/79, 12/104 (with picture),
    14/90-91 (with pictures)
Kitten, A (Farjeon), 1/118
kneecap, 11/40 (with picture)
knee pad (equipment), 11/183
knife, 3/95 (picture), 8/16 (with
    picture)
koala, 4/36, 4/37, 4/182 (picture)
kola nut, 5/104 (with picture)
Korea, 12/104, 14/42, 14/75,
    14/145 (with picture)
Kosciuszko, Mount (Australia),
    13/25
Krak des Chevaliers (castle,
    Syria), 13/89 (with picture)
Kremlin (Moscow), 13/95 (picture)
Krikalev, Sergei
    Konstantinovich (cosmonaut),
    7/181 (picture)
Krishna (god), 14/63
Kuiper belt (comets), 7/104
kutyapi (musical instrument),
    3/124 (with picture)
Kwanzaa, 14/182 (with picture)

L

M

mining geologist (scientist), 6/44
mint (plant), 5/33, 5/136 (with
    picture), 5/137 (picture)
Mir (space station), 7/169 (picture)
mirage, 8/124-125 (with pictures)
mirror, 8/116 (with picture), 8/120-
    121 (with pictures), 8/127 (picture)
    hologram and, 9/32 (with picture)
    telescope, 7/147 (with picture),
    7/148
mission specialist (astronaut),
    7/172-173, 7/174, 7/181 (picture)
Miss Mary Mack (poem), 1/139
Missouri River (U.S.A.), 13/17
mistakes, 11/139, 11/177
mistletoe, 5/44 (with picture), 5/47
Mitchell, Lucy Sprague (poet)
    House of the Mouse, The, 1/115
mite, 4/145 (with picture)
Mitten Song, The (Allen), 1/39
mixer, electric, 9/46 (picture)
moat, of castle, 13/87, 13/90
    (with picture), 13/92 (picture)
mobile telephone, 9/84 (picture),
    9/102-103 (with picture), 9/109
    (picture), 12/151 (picture)
model (art), 3/96-97 (with pictures)
modem (machine), 9/98, 9/106,
    12/151
moeritherium (extinct animal),
    4/172 (with picture)
molecule, 8/54-55 (with pictures)
    form of matter and, 8/59, 8/88-91
        (with pictures), 8/100-103 (with
        pictures)
    in air, 6/109-110
    sound wave and, 8/142, 8/144
    temperature and, 8/86-103 (with
        pictures)
mollusc, 4/10, 4/25 (with pictures),
    4/110-113 (with pictures)
molten rock, 6/23
Monday's Child (Mother Goose),
    1/77
Mongolia, 12/12 (picture)
monkey, 4/24 (picture), 4/32
    (picture), 5/72 (with picture)
    black colobus, 4/179 (picture)
    poem about
        Monkeys and the Crocodile, The,
        1/128
    woolly spider, 4/166 (picture)
Monkey King, The (opera), 3/148
    (picture)
monkey puzzle (tree), 5/39
    (picture)
Monkeys and the Crocodile, The

(Richards), 1/128
monorail, 9/62
monsters, stories about
    Jack and the Beanstalk, 2/12-21
    Old Woman and Her Dumpling, The,
        2/48-57
    Three Billy Goats Gruff, The, 2/97-99
Montaigne, Michel de (author),
    13/86 (picture)
month, 14/14-19
Montreal (Canada), 13/114 (with
    picture)
Moomba (festival), 14/64-65 (with
    pictures)
moon, 6/106, 7/38-61 (with
    pictures)
    calendar and, 14/14-19, 14/30
    crescent, 7/42, 7/50 (with picture),
        7/53 (with picture)
    early beliefs about, 7/42-45 (with
        pictures), 7/142 (with picture)
    eclipses and, 7/26-27 (with
        pictures), 7/48 (with pictures)
    first person to visit, 7/166-167
        (with pictures)
    full, 7/51 (with picture), 7/52 (with
        picture)
    living on, 7/56-57 (with pictures)
    phases of, 7/50-53 (with pictures)
    poems about
        I See the Moon, 1/41
        Moon-Come-Out, 1/40
        Moon-in-Water, 1/85
    reflection of light by, 7/46-47 (with
        pictures), 8/116-117 (with
        picture)
    stories about
        Clever Frog, 2/118-123
        Why the Sun and the Moon Live in
            the Sky, 2/100-105
    surface of, 7/54-55 (with pictures)
    tides and, 7/58 (with pictures)
Moon-Come-Out (Farjeon), 1/40
Moon Festival, 14/145 (with
    picture)
Moon-in-Water (Eastwick), 1/85
moons, of planets, 7/60-61 (with
    pictures), 7/75, 7/81-89 (with
    pictures)
moonstone (gem), 6/33 (picture)
Moore, Lilian (poet)
    Snowy Morning, 1/38
Morisot, Berthe (artist), 3/54-55
    (with pictures)
morning glory, 5/43 (picture)
Morning Light (Friedrich), 3/57
    (picture)

Morocco, 12/126 (with picture),
    12/179 (picture), 13/78 (picture)
mosaic, 13/123, 13/124-125 (with
    picture)
mosaic (art), 10/40 (with picture)
Moscow (Russia), 13/95 (picture)
Moses (Michelangelo), 3/92 (picture)
Moses (prophet), 14/80, 14/102
mosque, 13/122-124 (with pictures)
mosquito, 4/130-131 (with pictures)
    sound of, 8/148 (with picture)
    story about
        Why Mosquitoes Buzz in People's
            Ears, 2/108-117
moss, 5/15 (with picture), 5/17
    reindeer, 5/83 (picture)
Moss, Jeff (poet)
    Your Nose Is Running, 1/23
moth, 4/18 (picture), 4/127, 4/153
mother, 11/108, 12/10, 12/12,
    14/94-95 (with picture)
    baby's birth and, 11/92, 11/94-95
    genes from, 11/100 (with pictures)
    growing child and, 11/116-117
        (with pictures)
    in family tree, 11/111 (with picture)
    see also parent
Mother, Mother, I Want Another
    (story), 2/140-147
Mother Goose
    Animal Alphabet, An, 1/54-63
    Baa, Baa Black Sheep, 1/105
    Barber, Barber, 1/23
    Bell Horses, 1/81
    Clock, The, 1/81
    Diddle, Diddle, Dumpling, 1/43
    Diller, a Dollar, A, 1/81
    Doctor Foster Went to Gloucester,
        1/36
    Donkey, Donkey, 1/95
    Early to Bed and Early to Rise, 1/45
    Georgie Porgie, 1/17
    Hey, Diddle, Diddle, 1/104
    Hickety, Pickety, My Black Hen,
        1/105
    Hickory, Dickory, Dock, 1/80
    Higglety, Pigglety, Pop!, 1/14
    Hoddley, Poddley, 1/101
    Hot Cross Buns, 1/32
    House That Jack Built, The, 1/18-19
    Humpty Dumpty, 1/22
    Hush, Baby, My Doll, 1/43
    Hush-a-Bye Baby, 1/43
    If All the World Were Paper, 1/32
    I Had a Little Hobby Horse, 1/104
    I Saw a Ship, 1/98
    I See the Moon, 1/41

N

n (letter), rhyme about, 1/59
nail (fastener), 8/18-19
nail (part of body), see fingernail; toenail
name
  family, 12/14-17 (with pictures)
  first, 12/14 (with picture), 12/18-19 (with pictures)
  stories about
    Bunyip of Berkeley's Creek, The, 2/159-165
    Prince and the Orphan, The, 2/74-87
  tribal, 12/26
name day, 14/11
name tag, for baby, 11/97 (with picture)
Namibia, 6/154 (picture)
nanny (caregiver), 15/92-93
narwhal, 4/49
NASA, see National Aeronautics and Space Administration
nasturtium, 5/95 (with picture), 5/99 (picture)
National Aeronautics and Space Administration, 7/79, 7/172, 7/174, 7/183
National Day, 14/150 (picture)
national monument, 13/108-109 (with pictures)
national park, 4/180-181, 13/116-117, 13/121
Native Americans, see Indians, American
naturalist (scientist), 4/183 (with picture), 6/180
natural resources, 6/42
  protecting, 6/158-163 (with pictures), 6/170-179 (with pictures)
Nature Note (Guiterman), 1/106
Navajo (people), 7/141 (with picture), 12/113 (picture)
navel, 11/95
Ndebele (people), 13/71 (picture)
Ndudu, Lake (Tanzania), 6/97 (picture)
nebula, 7/120 (with picture)
necklace, 10/82-83 (with pictures), 12/32 (picture)
nectar, 4/134, 5/27, 5/103, 5/150
needle, 8/8, 8/16

neighbour, 12/9 (with pictures), 12/35-41 (with pictures), 12/117, 12/170
neighbourhood, 12/35-41 (with pictures)
neighbourhood map (project), 13/134-135 (with pictures)
Nelson, Horatio (British admiral), 13/109 (with picture)
Nepal, 13/121, 14/63
Neptune (planet), 7/64 (picture), 7/86-87 (with picture), 7/90 (with picture)
nerve, 11/62-63 (with picture)
  in smelling, 11/81
  in touch, 11/86-87 (with picture)
  pain and, 11/86-87 (with picture), 11/121, 11/152-153 (with picture)
nest
  bird, 4/52-53 (with pictures)
  chimpanzee, 4/41 (picture)
  squirrel, 4/41 (picture)
  wood ant, 4/132-133 (with picture)
Netherlands, 12/51 (picture), 12/123, 12/134 (picture), 12/179, 14/92, 14/129
  barge children in, 12/123 (with picture)
  feast of St. Nicholas in, 14/174, 14/175 (with picture)
  nursery rhyme from
    It's Snowing, It's Blowing, 1/37
network, computer, 9/106-107 (with picture)
Neuschwanstein (castle, Germany), 13/93 (with picture)
New Delhi (India), 14/34-35
New England (U.S.A.), 6/154 (picture)
Newfoundland and Labrador, 12/39 (picture)
New Guinea, 12/32 (picture)
Newman, James H. (astronaut), 7/181 (picture)
New Orleans (U.S.A.), 14/53 (picture)
news, 12/149-151 (with pictures)
newspaper, 12/149 (with pictures)
newt, 4/82 (picture), 4/88
Newton, Isaac (scientist), 7/156 (with picture)
New Year, Chinese, 14/26, 14/42 (with picture)
New Year's Day, 14/24-27 (with pictures)
New Year Tree, 14/24

New York City (New York), 13/53 (picture), 14/61
  skyscrapers in, 13/110, 13/112 (with picture)
  theatre in, 3/146, 3/163 (picture)
New Zealand, 6/87 (picture), 12/56, 13/24
  power station in, 8/80-81 (picture)
  special days in, 14/86, 14/115, 14/166, 14/181
  Waitangi Day, 14/44 (with picture)
  sun myth from, 7/30
  woodcarving in, 3/10
  see also Maori
Niagara Falls (North America), 13/117 (with picture)
Niagara River (North America), 6/85 (picture)
Nicholas, St. (Christian saint), 14/174-175 (with pictures)
Nigeria, 12/135 (picture), 13/15
  National Day in, 14/150 (with picture)
Night (McKay), 1/50
night, poems about
  Good Night, 1/50
  Night, 1/50
  Night, The, 1/50
  Water Bug, The, 1/51
  see day and night
Night, The (poem), 1/50
nightshade, 5/44 (with picture)
Nile River (Africa), 6/86, 13/15
nitrogen, 6/109
  in air, 7/73
Nobel Prize, 8/57
noh play, 3/149
noise, 8/158-159 (with picture)
nonagon (shape), 10/37 (picture)
Nootka Indians, 3/94-95 (with pictures)
north (direction), 13/136-137, 13/146
North America, 6/49 (pictures), 13/10 (with picture), 13/16-17 (with pictures), 13/19, 13/100
  customs in, 12/24-25
  dessert in, 12/59
  natural wonders of, 13/117 (with picture), 13/119 (with picture)
  see also specific countries
northern forest community, 5/68-71 (with pictures)
Northern Hemisphere, 7/24, 7/114-116 (with picture), 13/150-151, 14/108, 14/111, 14/123

o (letter), rhyme about, 1/59
oak, 5/12 (picture), 5/59 (with picture)
oak leaf, 14/89 (picture)
oarweed, 5/52 (picture)
oasis, 6/66
oats, 5/90 (with picture), 12/47
Oberon (moon), 7/61 (picture)
observatory, 7/151 (with pictures)
obsidian (rock), 6/23
ocean, 6/72-83 (with pictures)
  beach and, 6/80-81 (with pictures)
  climate of, 6/153
  energy from, 8/80-81
  floor of, 6/68-69 (with picture)
  food from, 12/54-55 (with pictures)
  mountains in, 6/69 (with picture)
  oil formed in, 6/40-41 (with pictures)
  on Uranus, 7/85 (with picture)
  poems about
    Ayii, Ayii, 1/87
    By the Sandy Water, 1/85
  salt in, 6/78 (with picture)
  shaping land, 6/83 (with picture)
  story about
    Thousand Pails of Water, A, 2/181-189
  tectonic plates and, 6/49 (with picture)
  waves in, 6/76-77 (with picture), 6/80
Oceania (region), 13/24
ocean liner (ship), 13/45 (with picture)
oceanographer (scientist), 4/183, 6/100-101 (with picture)
octagon (shape), 10/37 (picture), 10/40 (picture)
octave, 3/134
October, 14/146-157 (with pictures)
  birthdays in, 14/148-149 (with pictures)
  birthstone for, 6/33 (picture)
octopus, 4/25 (picture), 4/110, 4/112-113 (with pictures), 12/60 (picture)
oesophagus, 11/53
Oh! Look at the Moon (Follen), 7/51
Oh Where Has My Little Dog Gone? (poem), 1/100

oil, 8/73
  crude, see petroleum
oil rig, 6/40-41 (pictures), 6/96 (picture)
oil spill, 4/175 (with picture), 4/180-181 (with picture), 6/177 (with picture)
Oksapmin (people), 10/71
Old King Cole (Mother Goose), 1/20
Old Mother Hubbard (Mother Goose), 1/34-35
old people, stories about
  Glooscap and His People, 2/130-137
  Old Woman and Her Dumpling, The, 2/48-57
  Thousand Pails of Water, A, 2/181-189
Old Woman and Her Dumpling, The (story), 2/48-57
oleander, 5/44 (with picture)
olive, 5/99 (picture), 12/52 (picture)
Olympic Games, 12/92-93 (with pictures), 12/182 (picture)
Olympus Mons (Mars), 7/75
ombu tree, 5/177
omnivore, 4/13
Once I Saw a Little Bird (poem), 1/110
One for Anger (Mother Goose), 1/64
One for the Money (Mother Goose), 1/64
One Thing at a Time (poem), 1/89
One, Two, Buckle My Shoe (Mother Goose), 1/66
1, 2, 3, 4 (Mother Goose), 1/64
1, 2, 3, 4, 5 ! (Mother Goose), 1/64
onion, 5/33, 5/97 (with picture), 5/99 (picture), 5/119 (picture)
Onitsura (poet), 1/164
Oort cloud, 7/104
opal (gem), 6/32 (with picture)
opera, 3/148 (with picture), 3/150-151 (with picture)
opossum, 4/37 (with picture), 4/149
optical fibre, 9/99 (with picture)
orange (colour), 6/106-107, 8/128, 8/131
orange (fruit), 5/104 (picture)
orangutan, 4/179, 5/72 (picture)
orbit, 8/45-47 (with pictures)
  of artificial satellite, 7/160, 7/162 (picture)

  of earth, 6/12-13 (with picture), 7/73
  of planets, 7/64, 7/143 (with pictures)
  of Pluto, 7/89
orchestra, 3/110-111 (with picture), 3/136-137 (with picture)
orchestra pit, 3/150-151 (picture)
orchid, 5/75, 5/170 (with picture)
ore, 6/34-35 (with picture), 9/139
Oregon (U.S.A.), 6/95 (picture)
organ (musical instrument), 3/122
organ, human, 11/43
  see also specific organs
organism, 5/11
origami, 3/14-17 (with pictures)
oriole, 4/53 (picture)
Orion (constellation), 7/112 (with picture), 7/113
Osaka Castle (Japan), 13/92
ostrich, 4/54 (picture), 4/55 (picture), 4/144 (with picture)
Our Children's Earth (verse), 1/84
outer core, of earth, 6/21
outhouse, 5/154 (with picture)
ovary, 11/59
ovenbird, rufous, 4/52 (picture)
owl, 4/162 (with picture)
  great horned, 4/51 (picture)
  poems about
    Owl and the Pussycat, The, 1/130-131
    Wise Old Owl, The, 1/112
Owl and the Pussycat, The (Lear), 1/130-131
Owl Hooted, The (song), 1/40
owl piñata (project), 3/102-103 (with pictures)
Oxenbury, Helen (author)
  It's My Birthday, 2/148-157
oxidizer, 9/78, 9/79
oxpecker (bird), 4/157 (picture)
oxygen
  as fuel, 9/78
  from plants, 5/112-113 (with pictures)
  in compounds, 8/53, 8/55
  in earth's air, 6/109, 7/73
  in human body, 11/47, 11/48, 11/51
  on Mars, 7/73
oyster, 4/110, 4/111

P

potter's wheel, **9**/47 *(picture)*, **9**/132 *(picture)*

pottery, **9**/132-133 *(with pictures)*

pouch (body part), **4**/36-37

Poussin, Nicolas (artist), **3**/66-67 *(with pictures)*

powder paint, **3**/42, **3**/43

power (energy), see **energy**

power plant, **6**/178, **8**/80-81 *(picture)*, **8**/170

Prague (Czech Republic), **9**/62 *(picture)*

prairie, **5**/62

prairie dog, **5**/60 *(picture)*

praise, for child, **15**/58

Prancing Pony, The (nursery rhyme), **1**/94

Prayer of the Little Ducks Who Went into the Ark, The (de Gasztold), **1**/126

Praying Jew, The (Chagall), **3**/56 *(picture)*

precious stone, see **gem**

predator, **4**/62, **4**/148-149

prehistoric animal, **4**/168-173 *(with pictures)* see also **dinosaur**

prehistoric art, **3**/40-41 *(with pictures)*

Prelutsky, Jack (poet) *Bees,* **1**/117 *Hummingbird, The,* **1**/111

preschool, **15**/54, **15**/62

preschool child, **15**/46-63 *(with pictures)* development of, **15**/49 disciplining, **15**/56-58 *(with picture)* education of, **15**/50-54 *(with picture)* enjoying, **15**/62-63 health of, **15**/59-61 *(with picture)* problems of, **15**/55-58 *(with picture)* safety of, **15**/60-61

pressure, water, **9**/64-65

pretending, by animals, **4**/148-149 *(with pictures)*

prey, **4**/62, **4**/94, **4**/96, **4**/122, **4**/137

primary colour, **3**/46 *(with picture)*

prime meridian, **13**/153 *(with picture)*

Prince and the Orphan, The (story), **2**/74-87

princes and princesses, stories about *Cinderella,* **2**/60-73 *Prince and the Orphan, The,* **2**/74-87

printer (machine), **9**/39 *(with picture)*

prism, **8**/128 *(with picture)*

proboscis (body part), **4**/12

processed food, **9**/116-123 *(with pictures)*

producer, in food chain, **4**/163

product map, **13**/130 *(with picture)*

program, computer, **9**/39, **9**/106

projects, see **activities**

prokaryotes kingdom, **5**/10 *(picture)*

Prokofiev, Sergei (composer), **3**/130-131 *(with picture)*

prop (theatre), **3**/148

propeller aeroplane, **9**/74, **9**/81 *(with picture)* helicopter, **9**/72 *(with pictures)*, **9**/80 *(with picture)*

protein, in diet, **11**/158, **11**/160, **11**/169

protist kingdom, **5**/10 *(picture)*

proverb, **1**/169, **1**/182-183

puberty, **15**/85, **15**/90

Puebla (Mexico), **3**/20

Puerto Rico, **14**/29 *(with picture)*, **14**/86 proverb from, **1**/182 story from *Compae Rabbit's Ride,* **2**/124-129

Puffin, The (Wood), **1**/129

puffin (bird), poem about *Puffin, The,* **1**/129

pulley, **8**/22-23 *(with pictures)*

pulling, **8**/28, **8**/67, **8**/68 by gravity, **8**/41 by magnet, **8**/38-39, **8**/170 with pulley, **8**/22-23 see also **force; lifting**

pulsar, **7**/134

pulse, **11**/47 *(with picture)*

pump, **8**/68

pumping station, **9**/113 *(with picture)*

punishment, for child, **15**/107

pupa, **4**/128 *(with picture)*

pupil (part of eye), **11**/71 *(with picture)*

puppet, **3**/166-175 *(with pictures)*, **11**/124-125 *(with pictures)*, **12**/100 *(picture)*

Purple Cow, The (Burgess), **1**/75

pushchair, **9**/46 *(picture)*

pushing, **8**/28, **8**/67, **8**/68 by electrons in electric current, **8**/169-173 *(with pictures)* by heat energy, **8**/73, **8**/96, **8**/99 by magnet, **8**/39, **8**/170 by wedge, **8**/16-17 *(with pictures)* equilibrium and, **8**/40-41 *(with pictures)* inertia and, **8**/30-31 see also **force; lifting**

Pussycat, Pussycat (Mother Goose), **1**/99

pyramid, **13**/115 *(with picture)*

pyramids, of Egypt, **3**/90 *(with picture)*, **13**/15 *(with picture)*, **13**/103 *(with picture)*

pyrite, **8**/50 *(picture)*

python, **4**/67 *(picture)*, **4**/68 *(picture)* green, **4**/75 *(with picture)* reticulate, **4**/144 *(with picture)*

Q

R

r (letter), rhyme about, **1**/60
rabbit, **4**/155 *(picture)*, **4**/162 *(with picture)*, **5**/56 *(picture)*, **5**/168-169
in art, **3**/71-73 *(with pictures)*
poems about
Here Is a Bunny, **1**/136
Rabbit, The, **1**/107
stories about
Compae Rabbit's Ride, **2**/124-129
Hare and the Tortoise, The, **1**/173
Rabbit, The (Roberts), **1**/107
raccoon, **4**/13 *(picture)*
radar, **9**/94-95, **9**/97
Doppler, **6**/147
radiation
from space, **7**/134-135 *(with picture)*
on Jupiter, **7**/81
radio, **9**/10 *(picture)*, **9**/86 *(with pictures)*
radio-controlled car (toy), **9**/93, **9**/109 *(picture)*
radiosonde (instrument), **6**/147
radio transmitter, **9**/86, **9**/97, **9**/102-103
radio wave
in radio, **9**/86
in remote control, **9**/93
in telephone system, **9**/99, **9**/102-103
in television, **9**/89
satellite as transmitter of, **9**/104-105 *(with picture)*
see also **radar**
radish, **5**/97 *(with picture)*, **5**/99 *(picture)*, **5**/138 *(with picture)*, **12**/52 *(picture)*
radium, **8**/56-57 *(with pictures)*
radius, of circle, **10**/27 *(with picture)*
rafflesia, **5**/167 *(with picture)*
railway, *see* **train**
rain, **6**/134-141 *(with pictures)*
acid, *see* **acid rain**
desert, **6**/65
flooding from, **6**/90-91 *(with pictures)*
hail and, **6**/144-145
hurricane, **6**/120, **6**/121
poems about
Doctor Foster Went to Gloucester, **1**/36
Rain, Rain, **1**/36

Rain on the Green Grass, **1**/37
rainbow and, **6**/138-139
Rain, Rain (Mother Goose), **1**/36
rainbow, **6**/138-139 *(with pictures)*, **8**/132-133
rain forest, tropical, **4**/175, **5**/72-75 *(with pictures)*, **13**/19, **13**/117
destruction of, **5**/172-173 *(with pictures)*, **6**/176-177 *(with picture)*
rain gauge (project), **6**/136-137 *(with pictures)*
Rain on the Green Grass (Mother Goose), **1**/37
Ramadan, **14**/30-31 *(with pictures)*
Ramírez de Arellano, Rafael (author)
Compae Rabbit's Ride, **2**/124-129
ramp, **8**/15
Ramphorhynchus (extinct reptile), **4**/168 *(picture)*
rancher, **4**/183
ranger, **4**/183
rapid (river), **6**/85 *(with picture)*
rat
kangaroo, **4**/41 *(picture)*
poem about
Three Young Rats, **1**/113
raw materials, **9**/110 *(with picture)*
Re (god), **7**/30 *(with picture)*
reading
about places, **13**/62, **13**/64-69, **13**/169
to preschool children, **15**/19, **15**/51-52 *(with picture)*
to school-age child, **15**/72, **15**/83
Reason, The (Aldis), **1**/129
reasoning, with child, **15**/57-58
receptionist, **13**/178-179 *(with picture)*
recipes, **12**/70-77 *(with pictures)*
breakfast sundae, **11**/164-165 *(with pictures)*
bruschetta, **12**/72-73 *(with pictures)*
crunchies, **5**/104 *(with picture)*
date bars, **12**/76-77 *(with pictures)*
fufu, **12**/74-75 *(with pictures)*
ice cream, **9**/124-125 *(with pictures)*, **14**/120 *(with pictures)*
lemonade, **12**/70-71 *(with picture)*
pizza, **11**/167 *(with pictures)*
punch, **14**/28
rice cakes, **14**/50 *(with picture)*
salad, **5**/98-101 *(with pictures)*
snack kebab, **11**/166 *(with pictures)*
sweet apple slices, **14**/141 *(with picture)*

picture)
recreation, *see* **game; sports**
rectangle (shape), **10**/9-11 *(with pictures)*, **10**/36 *(picture)*
making from squares (exercise), **10**/25 *(with picture)*
tangram (exercise), **10**/32-33 *(with pictures)*
rectum, **11**/55 *(with picture)*
recumbent bicycle, **9**/51 *(with picture)*
recycling
paper, **9**/127-129 *(with pictures)*
rain, **6**/134-135 *(with pictures)*
resources, **5**/111, **5**/182, **6**/163, **6**/175 *(with picture)*, **6**/182-183 *(with pictures)*
red (colour), **6**/106-107, **8**/128, **8**/131, **8**/133, **9**/89-90
red blood cell, **11**/48 *(picture)*, **11**/49 *(picture)*
Red Bottle (Cragg), **3**/100 *(picture)*
redwood, **5**/38 *(with picture)*
reed (plant), **5**/107 *(with pictures)*
reef, coral, *see* **coral reef**
reflection
light, **7**/46-47 *(with pictures)*, **7**/64, **8**/116-117 *(with pictures)*, **8**/120-121 *(with pictures)*, **8**/128, **8**/129
sound, **8**/152-155
reflective nebula, **7**/120 *(with picture)*
refrigerator, **9**/16-17 *(with pictures)*
refugee camp, **12**/180
rehearsal, **3**/152-153
reindeer, **12**/50 *(with picture)*, **13**/43 *(with picture)*
religion
buildings and, **13**/122-125 *(with pictures)*
food and, **12**/57
see also specific religions
religious dance, **3**/178
Remembrance Day, **14**/166-167 *(with pictures)*
remote control, **9**/84 *(picture)*, **9**/92-93 *(with pictures)*, **9**/109 *(picture)*
reproduction, **5**/10
human, **11**/59, **11**/92-93 *(with pictures)*
reproduction, plant
without seeds, **5**/32-33 *(with pictures)*
with seeds, **5**/20-29 *(with pictures)*

s

s (letter), rhyme about, 1/60
Sacrifice, Festival of, 14/93
Sadiki (fictional character), 3/154-159 *(with pictures)*
sadness, 11/123-125 *(with pictures)*, 11/140-141
safety
  at home, 11/180-181 *(with pictures)*
  away from home, 11/182-183 *(with pictures)*
  for preschool children, 15/50, 15/60-61, 15/100-101
  for school-age child, 15/74-75 *(with picture)*, 15/100-101
  in sports, 12/95 *(with pictures)*
  traffic signs, 12/144-145 *(with pictures)*
sage, 5/136 *(picture)*, 5/137 *(picture)*
Sahara Desert (Africa), 13/14, 13/15, 13/118 *(with picture)*, 13/162 *(picture)*
  clothes for, 13/74-75 *(with picture)*
  travel on, 13/48-49 *(picture)*
sailfish, 4/11
sailing boat, 13/44 *(picture)*
St. John's Day, 14/108 *(with picture)*
St. John's Fire, 14/108
St. Joseph's Day, 14/66 *(with picture)*
St. Patrick's Day, 14/61 *(with picture)*
St. Peter's Basilica (Rome), 13/125 *(with picture)*
saint's day, 14/11
salad, 5/98-101 *(with pictures)*
salamander, 4/21 *(picture)*, 4/24 *(picture)*, 4/88-89 *(with pictures)*
  giant, 4/145 *(with picture)*
  red, 4/88 *(picture)*
  spotted, 4/66 *(picture)*
Salazar, Violet (author)
  Squares Are Not Bad, 11/132-137
saliva, 11/53
saliva gland, 11/55 *(picture)*, 11/106 *(with picture)*
salmon, 4/160 *(with picture)*
salt, 6/26 *(picture)*
  in ocean, 6/78 *(with picture)*
saltiness, 11/82 *(with picture)*
saltpetre (fuel), 9/79
saltwater community, 5/64-67 *(with pictures)*

salvia, red (plant), 5/140 *(picture)*
Salyut I (space laboratory), 7/168 *(picture)*
Samals (people), 3/30
San (people), 7/28 *(with picture)*, 7/45 *(with picture)*
sand, 9/110
  beach, 6/81
  desert, 6/64 *(with picture)*, 6/67 *(with picture)*
  in glassmaking, 9/136
  travelling on, 13/48-49 *(with picture)*
sand bar, 6/83 *(with picture)*
sand castle, 8/50-51 *(with picture)*
sand dollar, 4/120 *(with picture)*
sand pillar (wind), 6/123
sandstone, 6/24 *(with picture)*
Santa Claus, 14/174, 14/180 *(with picture)*
São Francisco River (Brazil), 6/90 *(picture)*
sap, 5/103
sapphire, 6/32-33 *(with pictures)*
sardine, 4/96
sardonyx (gem), 6/33 *(picture)*
sargassum weed, 5/53
sari (clothes), 12/26 *(with picture)*
sashimi (food), 12/55 *(with picture)*
satellite, 7/41
  see also **moon; moons, of planets**
satellite, artificial, 7/158, 7/160-163 *(with pictures)*, 8/44-45 *(with pictures)*, 9/104-105 *(with picture)*, 12/150
  weather, 6/146
satellite dish, 9/84 *(picture)*, 9/89 *(with picture)*, 9/109 *(picture)*
Saturn (planet), 7/61, 7/64 *(picture)*, 7/82-83 *(with picture)*, 7/91 *(with picture)*
Saturn V (rocket), 9/79
saucepan, boiling, 8/98-99 *(with picture)*
Saudi Arabia, 12/51, 12/179, 13/29 *(picture)*, 13/124 *(with picture)*, 14/93
savanna, 5/62
savory (spice), 5/136 *(with picture)*
saw, 8/16 *(with picture)*
saxifrage, alpine (plant), 5/87 *(with picture)*
Say Well and Do Well (poem), 1/89
scab, 11/149
scale (body part), 4/76, 4/90

scale (machine), 10/166-167 *(with pictures)*
scale (map), 13/140-145 *(with pictures)*
scale (music), 3/134-135 *(with picture)*
scallop, 4/25 *(picture)*, 4/110-111 *(with picture)*
Scandinavia, 12/53
scar, 11/149
scenery (theatre), 3/150-151 *(picture)*
school, 12/118-125 *(with pictures)*
  behaviour problems in, 15/104
  disabled child in, 15/109-111, 15/115-116 *(with picture)*
  early years of, 15/70-73 *(with pictures)*
  entering new, 15/97
  feelings about, 11/119 *(with picture)*, 15/79-81
  graduation from, 12/22 *(with picture)*
  health problems in, 15/75-76
  preschool children and, 15/54
  safety in travel to and from, 15/74-75 *(with picture)*
  see also **education; preschool**
school (fish), 4/94 *(with picture)*
school-age child, 15/64-83 *(with pictures)*
  development of, 15/65-68 *(with pictures)*
  early school years of, 15/69-73 *(with pictures)*
  enjoying, 15/82-83
  health of, 15/75-76
  safety of, 15/74-75 *(with picture)*
science, in school, 15/72
scissors, 8/16
Scorpio (constellation), 7/110 *(with picture)*
scorpion, 4/137 *(with picture)*
Scotland, 12/29 *(picture)*, 14/74
  Highland Games in, 14/115 *(with picture)*
  New Year in, 14/24-25 *(with picture)*
scraper box (machine), 9/170-171 *(with picture)*
screw, 8/18-19 *(with pictures)*
screwdriver, 8/8
scrotum, 11/59
sculpture, 3/79-105 *(with pictures)*
  assemblage, 3/101 *(with pictures)*
  clay, 3/80-89 *(with pictures)*

water, 4/158 (picture)
see also cobra; python
snapdragon, 5/141 (picture)
snapper, red (fish), 14/26
sneeze, 11/146 (with picture),
11/179
snout, 4/47 (with picture)
snow, 6/135, 6/142-143 (with
pictures)
hail and, 6/144
poems about
A Lost Snowflake, 1/37
Cynthia in the Snow, 1/39
It's Blowing, It's Snowing, 1/37
Snowy Morning, 1/38
Thaw, 1/38
travel across, 13/42-43 (with
pictures)
snowflake, 6/143 (with picture)
snow leopard mask (project),
14/76-77 (with pictures)
Snow Maiden (tradition), 14/24
(picture)
snowmobile, 13/42-43 (with
picture)
Snowy Morning (Moore), 1/38
soap, 9/130-131 (with pictures)
soccer, 12/90-91 (with picture)
social studies, 15/72
soil, 4/163, 4/165
Sojourner (robot), 7/77 (with
picture)
Sol (god), 7/10
"solar," meaning of, 7/10, 8/71
solar cell, 8/70 (picture)
solar energy, 7/14-17 (with
pictures), 8/65, 8/70-71 (with
pictures), 8/113, 8/115
solar house, 8/70-71 (with picture)
solar panel, 7/163 (picture)
solar system, 7/10, 7/62-97 (with
pictures)
comets in, 7/104
early views of, 7/142-143 (with
picture)
see also moon; planet; sun
solar telescope, 7/36
solar wind, 7/105
solid (physics), 6/108, 8/58-63 (with
pictures)
melting of, 8/88-89 (with pictures)
sound waves and, 8/144-145 (with
picture)
solid shape, see shape
Solomon Grundy (Mother Goose),
1/76
Solomon Islands, 12/99

Somewhere (poem), 13/177
song, 3/138-139 (with picture)
Song of the Frog, The (nursery
rhyme), 1/49
Song of the Train (McCord), 1/24
sonic boom, 8/151
Sonoran Desert (Mexico), 13/17
sorghum, 5/90
sorrel, 5/83 (picture)
sorting, with Venn diagram,
10/74-78 (with pictures)
sound, 6/105, 8/139-159 (with
pictures)
bouncing, 8/152-155 (with pictures)
by voice box, 11/74-75
hearing, 11/76-77
loudness of, 8/156-157 (with
picture)
measuring, 8/156-157 (with picture)
movement and, 8/139 (with
picture), 8/150-151 (with
picture)
on moon, 7/57
pitch of, 8/148-149 (with picture)
recording of, 9/28-31 (with
pictures)
see also ear; hearing; vibration,
sound; wave
soup, 12/61 (picture)
sourness (taste), 11/82 (with
picture)
south (direction), 13/136-137
South Africa, 3/113 (picture),
13/15
South America, 6/49 (with
pictures), 12/56 (picture), 12/91,
13/10 (with picture), 13/16,
13/18-19 (with pictures), 13/100-
101
Bolívar's birthday in, 14/121 (with
picture)
Columbus Day in, 14/152-153
(with picture)
natural wonders of, 13/116-117
(with pictures)
see also specific countries
Southern Hemisphere, 7/24,
7/114-116 (with picture), 7/131,
13/150-151, 14/111, 14/123
South Pole, 6/11, 6/71, 7/24,
7/73, 7/137, 13/20-21, 13/136
climate at, 6/152, 6/169
south pole (magnet), 8/38-39 (with
pictures)
South Tyrol (Austria), 13/38 (with
picture)
souvenir, 13/174-175 (with pictures)

Soviet Union, 3/130-131
space programme of, 7/168 (with
pictures)
see also cosmonaut
Soyuz (spacecraft), 7/169 (with
picture)
space
orbiting in, 8/46-47 (with pictures)
satellite in, 8/44-45 (with pictures)
travelling in, see space travel
space, in sculpture, 3/98 (with
picture)
Space Camp, U.S., 7/173 (picture)
space probe, 7/69, 7/71, 7/77,
7/183 (with picture)
space shuttle, 7/170-171 (with
pictures), 7/174 (picture), 7/178
(picture), 7/179, 7/181 (picture)
space station, 7/168-169 (with
pictures)
space suit, 7/175 (picture)
space travel
by rocket, 9/34
careers in, 7/172-173 (with picture)
to Mars, 7/78-79 (with pictures)
to moon, 7/167-168 (with pictures)
training for, 7/174-176 (with
pictures)
see also astronaut; launches
spacewalk, first, 7/165
Spain, 14/95, 14/142
Columbus Day in, 14/152-153
food in, 12/56 (picture), 12/58
games in, 12/82 (with picture),
12/84
learning in, 12/114-115 (with
picture)
proverbs from, 1/182, 1/183
St. Joseph's Day in, 14/66 (with
picture)
Spanish (language), 10/49
spark plug, 9/57 (with picture)
sparrow, 4/59 (with picture), 4/61
(with picture)
speaking, 3/112-113 (with pictures),
11/60 (picture), 11/74-75 (with
pictures)
hearing problems and, 11/79
speech, see language; speaking
speech-reading, 11/79
sperm, 11/92 (with picture), 11/94,
11/100
sphere (shape), 10/11 (with picture),
10/42 (picture)
sphinx, see Great Sphinx
spice, 5/103

U

u (letter), rhyme about, 1/61
Uganda, 13/39 *(picture)*
Ukraine, 3/130, 14/79 *(pictures)*
ultraviolet rays, 7/36, 7/183, 8/133 *(with picture)*
Uluru (Australia), 13/24-25, 162 *(picture)*
umbilical cord, 11/95 *(with picture),* 11/96
umbrella, 9/149 *(picture)*
UN, *see* **United Nations**
uncle, 11/109, 11/111 *(with picture),* 12/10, 15/62
underachiever, 15/80
UNICEF, 14/156, 15/117
unicycle, 9/51 *(with picture)*
Union of Soviet Socialist Republics, *see* **Soviet Union**
uniqueness
of human face, 11/11
of people, 11/130-131
United Kingdom, 12/41 *(picture),* 12/169, 13/92, 13/99, 14/45, 14/166
cricket in, 12/91 *(with picture)*
etiquette in, 12/160-161 *(with picture)*
food in, 12/53, 12/68 *(with picture),* 12/69
independence from, 14/32, 14/44, 14/114, 14/116, 14/151

school in, 12/121 *(picture)*
see also **England; Scotland; Wales**
United Nations, 12/182-183 *(with pictures)*
on rights of children, 15/117-119
see also **UNICEF**
United Nations Day, 14/156-157 *(with pictures)*
United States of America, *see* **U.S.A.**
Unity, U.S. (spacecraft), 7/169 *(picture),* 7/178 *(picture),* 7/180 *(picture)*
universe
galaxies in, 7/130-131
number of stars in, 7/101
studying, 7/138-183 *(with pictures)*
see also specific topics, such as **planet**
uranium, 6/27 *(with picture)*
Uranus (planet), 7/61 *(picture),* 7/64 *(picture),* 7/84-85 *(with picture),* 7/86, 7/90 *(with picture)*
urethra, 11/57 *(with picture)*
urine, 11/56
Ursa Major (constellation), 7/98-99 *(picture),* 7/112 *(with picture)*
U.S.A., 13/16, 14/115, 14/183
clothing in, 12/31 *(picture)*
eating customs in, 12/66-67 *(with picture)*
family in, 12/11 *(picture),* 12/20 *(picture)*
food in, 12/56, 12/68 *(with picture)*

games in, 12/89, 12/91 *(with picture)*
kites in, 12/105 *(picture)*
language in, 12/128-129, 12/132
leader of, 12/178
learning in, 12/115, 12/126 *(with picture)*
measurement in, 10/163
special days in
April Fool's Day, 14/74
Christmas, 14/180
Columbus Day, 14/152
Father's Day, 14/105
Flag Day, 14/107
Halloween, 14/156 *(with picture)*
Independence Day, 14/116 *(with picture)*
Kwanzaa, 14/182 *(with picture)*
Martin Luther King, Jr., Day, 14/36-37 *(with pictures)*
Mother's Day, 14/94
Remembrance Day, 14/166-167
Thanksgiving, 14/168-169 *(with pictures)*
Valentine's Day, 14/45
toys in, 12/99 *(with picture),* 12/101 *(picture)*
traditions in, 12/24-26 *(with picture)*
uterus, 11/59
Utrillo, Maurice (artist), 3/59 *(with picture)*

185

V

v (letter), rhyme about, 1/62
vacuum, 9/23
vacuum cleaner, 9/22-23 *(with picture)*, 9/148 *(picture)*
vagina, 11/59, 11/96
Valencia (Spain), 14/66 *(with picture)*
Valentine, St. (Christian saint), 14/45 *(with picture)*
Valentine's Day, 14/45-47 *(with pictures)*
valley, 6/60-61 *(with pictures)*
  in ocean, 6/68 *(with picture)*
Vancouver (Canada), 14/114 *(picture)*
vanilla, 5/104
vanity, story about
  Emperor's New Clothes, The, 2/36-47
Vatican City, 13/23
Vega (star), 7/116, 14/126-127
vegetable, 11/159-163 *(with pictures)*, 12/52-53 *(with pictures)*, 12/61
vegetarian, 12/57
vein, 11/47 *(with picture)*
vein, in rock, 6/34 *(with picture)*
Venezuela, 14/121
  nursery rhyme from
  Lullaby to a Naughty Baby, 1/49
Venn diagram, 10/74-75 *(with pictures)*
vent
  house, 9/154 *(picture)*
  submarine, 9/70 *(with picture)*
Venus (goddess), 7/91 *(with picture)*
Venus (planet), 7/64 *(with picture)*, 7/70-71 *(with pictures)*, 7/91 *(with picture)*, 7/145 *(with picture)*
Venus'-flytrap, 5/49 *(with picture)*
Vermont (U.S.A.), 12/58 *(picture)*
Versailles, Palace of (France), 13/92-93 *(with picture)*
vertebrate, 4/108
Very Clumsy Click Beetle, The (Carle), 3/19 *(with picture)*
Very Hungry Caterpillar, The (Carle), 3/18 *(with picture)*

Veterans Day, 14/166-167
veterinary surgeon (vet), 4/182 *(with picture)*
vibration, sound, 8/140 *(with picture)*, 8/144, 8/147, 9/30-31, 9/86, 11/76
  in musical instrument, 3/115-122, 3/120-121
  in telephone diaphragm, 9/100-101
  loudness and, 8/157
  of vocal cords, 3/113
  pitch and, 8/148-149
Victoria (queen of Britain), 14/92 *(with picture)*
Victoria, Lake (Africa), 6/97
Victoria Day, 14/92 *(with picture)*
Victoria Falls (Africa), 13/15, 13/118 *(with picture)*
vicuña, 5/84
videocassette recorder, 9/35 *(picture)*
video game, 8/179 *(with pictures)*
video screen, 8/179
videotape, 9/29 *(with picture)*
Vietnam, 12/48, 14/42
viewfinder, of camera, 8/127 *(with picture)*
Viking 1 (spacecraft), 7/77
Viking 2 (spacecraft), 7/77
Vikings (people), 3/10 *(with picture)*
village family, 12/13 *(with picture)*
Villa Savoye (Poissy, France), 13/115
vine, 5/75 *(with picture)*
vinegar, 8/55
Vinson Massif (mountain, Antarctica), 13/21
vinyl, 9/141 *(with picture)*
violence, on television, 15/53, 15/66, 15/94
violet (colour), 8/131, 8/133
violin, 3/116 *(with picture)*
viper, 4/75
virtues, poems about
  Enjoy the Earth, 1/84
  Good, Better, Best, 1/89
  One Thing at a Time, 1/89
  Patience, 1/89
  Say Well and Do Well, 1/89
  Table Manners, 1/88

Thingumajigs, 1/90-91
Whatever You Do, 1/89
virus, 11/146-147
Vishnu (god), 13/125, 14/63 *(with picture)*
vision, *see* sight
vitamin, 11/159, 11/160, 11/169
vocal cords, 3/112-113 *(with picture)*, 11/74-75 *(with pictures)*
voice, 11/74-75
  see also speaking
voice box, *see* larynx
volcano, 6/18, 6/53-55 *(with pictures)*, 6/101 *(with picture)*, 7/86
  climate change and, 6/156-157 *(with picture)*
  Giant's Causeway, 6/28-29
  in ocean, 6/68 *(with picture)*
  island, 6/56-57 *(with pictures)*, 6/69 *(with picture)*
  lake, 6/95 *(picture)*
  rock from, 6/23
Volga River (Europe), 13/23
volleyball (sport), 12/91 *(picture)*
volume (measurement), 10/159 *(with picture)*, 10/170-171 *(with pictures)*
von Braun, Wernher (engineer), 7/158
vorticella (animal), 4/117 *(with picture)*
Voyager 1 (space probe), 7/81, 7/83
Voyager 2 (space probe), 7/81, 7/83, 7/85, 7/86
vulnerable animal, 4/179 *(with pictures)*
vulture, 4/165 *(picture)*, 4/178 *(picture)*

186

W

w (letter), rhyme about, 1/62

Wagner, Jenny (author)
Bunyip of Berkeley's Creek, The,
2/159-165

wagon, 8/20-21 *(with pictures),* 9/42 *(picture)*

Wailing Wall (Jerusalem), 14/103 *(picture)*

Waitangi Day, 14/44 *(with picture)*

Wales, 12/63

walkie-talkie, 9/109 *(picture)*

Walking (Glaubitz), 1/16

walking safely, 11/182-183, 15/74-75 *(with picture)*

wallaby, bridled nailtail, 4/179 *(picture)*

walnut, 5/104 *(picture)*

walrus, 4/46-47

"Waltzing Matilda" (song), 3/138-139 *(with picture)*

WAN (network), 9/106

Ward, Nathaniel (gardener), 5/128

warm-blooded animal, 4/24, 4/32, 4/158

warnings, by animals, 4/154-155 *(with pictures)*

washi (paper), 3/14-15 *(with pictures)*

washing, and health, 11/178-179

washing machine, 9/20-21 *(with pictures)*

Washington, D.C. (U.S.A.), 9/63 *(picture)*

Wash on Monday (Mother Goose), 1/76

waste
body, 11/48, 11/55, 11/56-57 *(with picture)*
removal in nature, 4/164-165 *(with pictures)*
see also **pollution**

watch, 9/35 *(picture)*

water
as compound, 8/53
as lens, 8/122 *(with picture)*
as liquid, 8/59
as natural resource, 6/162
as vapour, see **water vapour**
boiling, 8/88-89 *(with pictures)*
energy from, 8/67 *(with picture),* 8/80-81 *(with pictures)*
factory treatment of, 9/112-115 *(with pictures)*
floating on, 9/64-65 *(with pictures)*

health and, 11/159 *(picture)*
in toilet, 9/26-27 *(with picture)*
in washing machine, 9/20-21 *(with pictures)*
on earth, 6/18, 6/72 *(with picture),* 6/74-75
on Mars, 7/78
plants and, 5/40-41 *(with picture)*
pollution of, see **water pollution**
stories about
How the Turtle Saved His Own Life, 2/93-95
Old Woman and Her Dumpling, The, 2/48-57
Thousand Pails of Water, A, 2/181-189
Why the Sun and the Moon Live in the Sky, 2/100-105
testing sample, 6/100 *(with picture)*
travel across, 13/44-45 *(with pictures)*
underground, 6/98-99 *(with pictures)*
see also **liquid**

water buffalo, 12/50, 12/168-169 *(with picture)*

Water Bug, The (poem), 1/51

water chestnut, 5/99 *(picture)*

water colour, 3/42, 3/74-75 *(with pictures)*

water community, 5/64-67 *(with pictures)*

water dikkop (bird), 4/156

waterfall, 6/85 *(with picture),* 13/117-118 *(with pictures)*

water filter, 9/113-115 *(with pictures)*

waterfowl, 4/64-65 *(with pictures),* 4/175 *(picture)*

water level, 6/81 *(picture)*

water lily, 5/67 *(with picture)*

water pipe, in house, 9/155 *(picture)*

water pollution, 6/165, 6/166, 6/177 *(with picture)*

water survival training, 7/175 *(picture)*

water table, 6/98 *(with picture)*

water tower, 9/113 *(with picture)*

water vapour, 8/90-91 *(with pictures)*
in clouds, 6/125, 6/135
in fog, 6/128-129
in snow, 6/142

waterworks (factory), 9/113 *(with picture)*

wave

light, 8/118-119
ocean, 6/76-77 *(with picture),* 6/80
sound, 8/140-143 *(with pictures),* 8/148 *(with pictures)*

weather, 6/132-151 *(with pictures)*
folklore on, 6/148-149 *(with pictures)*
measuring (exercise), 10/176-177 *(with pictures)*
studying, 6/146-147 *(with pictures)*
see also **climate**

weather balloon, 6/147

weather forecast, 6/147 *(with picture)*

weather map, 13/130 *(with picture)*

weather station, 6/147, 6/150-151 *(with pictures)*

weaverbird, 4/53 *(picture)*

weaving, 12/113 *(picture),* 12/126, 13/76-77 *(with pictures)*

web, spider, 4/138-139 *(with pictures)*

wedding, see **marriage**

wedge, 8/16-17 *(with pictures)*

weed, 5/132, 5/133

Wee Little Worm, A (Riley), 1/104

Wee Willie Winkie (Mother Goose), 1/42

weight, 10/158 *(with picture)*
body, 11/154 *(with picture),* 15/69, 15/85, 15/88-89 *(picture)*
gravity, 7/57
measuring (exercises), 10/166-167 *(with pictures),* 10/173 *(with picture)*

weightlessness, 7/175, 8/46-47 *(with pictures)*

weightlifting, 12/92 *(picture)*

welwitschia, 5/79 *(picture),* 5/178-179 *(picture)*

west (direction), 13/136

Western Wall (Jerusalem), 13/122 *(with picture)*

West Indies, 12/88, 12/91 *(with picture)*

whale, 4/46, 4/48-49 *(with pictures),* 4/160
baleen, 4/13
beluga, 4/49
blue, 4/144 *(with picture)*
killer, 4/49
right, 4/48 *(picture)*
sperm, 4/49 *(with picture)*
story about
Thousand Pails of Water, A, 2/181-189

Whatever You Do (poem), 1/89

187

What Is Pink? (Rossetti), 1/74

wheat, 5/12 *(picture)*, **5**/91 *(picture)*, **12**/47 *(with picture)*

wheel, 8/20-21 *(with pictures)*, **13**/36-37 *(with pictures)*
gear, **8**/24-25 *(with pictures)*
in pulley, **8**/22 *(with picture)*

When Jacky's a Good Boy (poem), 1/88

Where Bananas Grow (poem), 1/102

Whisky Frisky (poem), 1/103

whistle, train, 8/150-151 *(with picture)*

white blood cell, 11/48 *(picture)*, **11**/49 *(picture)*

white dwarf, 7/118

White House (U.S.A.), **13**/94 *(picture)*

white light, 8/128-129

Who Is So Pretty? (Coatsworth), 1/114

Why Bear Has a Stumpy Tail (story), 2/106-107

Why Mosquitoes Buzz in People's Ears (story), 2/108-117

Why the Sun and the Moon Live in the Sky (story), 2/100-105

wide area network, 9/106 *(picture)*

width, of shape, 10/42 *(with picture)*

wildlife, *see* **animal**

wildlife reserve, 4/180-181

William the Conqueror (king of England), **13**/92

willow, 5/83 *(with picture)*, **5**/117
pussy, **4**/9 *(picture)*

Willow Leaves Murmur (nursery rhyme), 1/47

wind, 6/102 *(with picture)*, **6**/112-119 *(with pictures)*
dune and, **6**/67
energy from, **8**/67, **8**/68-69 *(with pictures)*
hail and, **6**/145
hurricane, **6**/120-121 *(with pictures)*
pollen and, **5**/26

tornado, **6**/122-123 *(with pictures)*

wind instrument, 3/118-121 *(with pictures)*

windmill, 8/68-69 *(with picture)*

window
house, **9**/153
security system and, **9**/97

windpipe (body part), **3**/113 *(picture)*

windsock (kite), **3**/11

wind sock (project), **6**/116-117 *(with pictures)*

Windsor Castle (England), **13**/92

wing
aeroplane, **8**/42-43 *(with pictures)*, **13**/54
bird, **4**/56-57 *(with pictures)*
insect, **4**/126-127 *(with picture)*

Winnipeg, Lake (Canada), **6**/96

winter, 5/56 *(with picture)*, **5**/80, **7**/22-25 *(with picture)*, **13**/151

wire
electrical, **8**/164-166 *(with picture)*, **8**/170
fibre-optic, **8**/136-137
sound wave in, **8**/145
see also **coil**

Wise Old Owl, The (poem), 1/112

wishing, poem about
Star-Light, Star-Bright, 1/40

witch, story about
Prince and the Orphan, The, 2/74-87

Witchhead Nebula, 7/121 *(picture)*

wolf, 4/155 *(with picture)*

wood, 5/34, **5**/110 *(with pictures)*, **9**/110
bridges of, **9**/160
in homes, **9**/152 *(with picture)*
paper from, **9**/126-127 *(with picture)*
sound and, **8**/131 *(picture)*

Wood, Robert Williams (poet)
Puffin, The, 1/129

woodcarving (craft), **3**/10 *(with picture)*, **3**/94-95 *(with pictures)*

woodchuck, 4/158-159 *(with picture)*

woodpecker, 4/61 *(with picture)*,

4/63 *(pictures)*

woodwind instrument, 3/118-119 *(with pictures)*, **3**/137

wool, 9/135 *(with picture)*

work, 13/78-79 *(with pictures)*
in community, **12**/170-171
sharing in family, **12**/166-169 *(with pictures)*
teaming up for, **12**/172-177 *(with pictures)*
see also **careers**

world
learning about the, **11**/116-117, **11**/120-121, **15**/50-51
people sharing, **12**/182-183
see also **Earth**

"World in a Day, The" (story), **13**/64-69 *(with pictures)*

World War I, 14/166-167 *(with pictures)*

World War II, 14/156, **14**/167

World Wide Web, 12/150, **12**/151
see also **Internet**

World Wide Fund for Nature, 5/179

worm, 4/21 *(picture)*, **4**/97 *(with picture)*, **4**/108, **4**/156

worship, 12/20 *(picture)*, **13**/122-125 *(with pictures)*

wrasse, 4/156 *(with picture)*

wren, 4/25 *(picture)*

Wright, Frank Lloyd (architect), **13**/115 *(with picture)*

Wright brothers (inventors), **12**/104

wrist bone, 11/102 *(with pictures)*

wrist guard, 11/183

writing, as skill, 15/68

writing activities, *see* **activities**

wrong, *see* **right and wrong**

WWF, *see* **World Wide Fund for Nature**

X

Y

Z

Illustration Acknowledgments

The Publishers of *Childcraft* gratefully acknowledge the courtesy of the following illustrators, photographers, agencies, and organizations for illustrations in this volume. When all the illustrations for a sequence of pages are from a single source, the inclusive page numbers are given. Credits should be read from top to bottom , left to right, on their respective pages. All illustrations are the exclusive property of the publishers of *Childcraft* unless names are marked with an asterisk (*).

Cover	Boys running through field—© Philip & Karen Smith, Tony Stone Images*; Boys on tire swing—© Lori Adamski-Peek, Tony Stone Images*; Tongan girl dancing—© Anna A. Zuckerman, Photo Edit*; African-American girl reading—© Cathy Melloan*	58-59	CHILDCRAFT photo
		62-63	© Grantpix, Monkmeyer*
		64-65	© Jon Feingersh, The Stock Market*; © Victoria Beller-Smith*
		66-67	© Don Smetzer, Tony Stone Images*
Back Cover	© Cathy Melloan*	68-69	© Lawrence Migdale*
1	© Lori Adamski-Peek, Tony Stone Images*; © Anna A. Zuckerman, Photo Edit*; © Cathy Melloan*	70-71	© Lawrence Migdale*
		72-73	CHILDCRAFT photo by Steve Hale; © David R. Frazier*
4-5	© Ariel Skelley, The Stock Market*; CHILDCRAFT photo by Steve Hale; CHILDCRAFT photo; © Lawrence Migdale*	74-75	CHILDCRAFT photo
		78-79	© Merrim, Monkmeyer*
		82-83	© Shackman, Monkmeyer*
6-7	© Lawrence Migdale*; © Victoria Beller-Smith*	84-85	© Jon Feingersh, The Stock Market*
8-9	CHILDCRAFT photo by Steven Spicer	90-91	CHILDCRAFT photo
10-11	CHILDCRAFT photo by Steven Spicer	94-95	© Cathy Melloan*
16-17	CHILDCRAFT photo by Steven Spicer	96-97	© Superstock*
34-35	CHILDCRAFT photo by Steven Spicer	98-99	© Jennie Woodcock, Corbis*
46-47	© Jon Feingersh, The Stock Market*	100-101	© Cathy Melloan*
48-49	© Jon Feingersh, The Stock Market*	102-103	© Armstrong, Zefa Picture Library*
50-51	© Eric Larravdieu, Tony Stone Images*; © Ariel Skelley, The Stock Market*	104-105	© David Young Wolff*
		108-109	© Mary Kate Denney, Tony Stone Images*
52-53	© Superstock*; © Grantpix, Monkmeyer*	112-113	© Cathy Melloan*
56-57	CHILDCRAFT photo	116-117	© Lawrence Migdale, Tony Stone Images*